Pronunciation for Advanced Learners of English

Teacher's Book

Pronunciation for Advanced Learners of English

Teacher's Book

David Brazil

CAMBRIDGE
UNIVERSITY PRESS

PUBLISHED BY THE PRESS SYNDICATE OF THE UNIVERSITY OF CAMBRIDGE
The Pitt Building, Trumpington Street, Cambridge, United Kingdom

CAMBRIDGE UNIVERSITY PRESS
The Edinburgh Building, Cambridge CB2 2RU, UK
40 West 20th Street, New York, NY 10011–4211, USA
477 Williamstown Road, Port Melbourne, VIC 3207, Australia
Ruiz de Alarcón 13, 28014 Madrid, Spain
Dock House, The Waterfront, Cape Town 8001, South Africa

http://www.cambridge.org

© Cambridge University Press 1994

First published 1994
Eighth printing 2003

Printed in the United Kingdom at the University Press, Cambridge

A *catalogue record for this book is available from the British Library*

ISBN 0 521 38799 X Teacher's Book
ISBN 0 521 38798 1 Student's Book
ISBN 0 521 38420 6 Set of 2 cassettes

Contents

Part 1: Notes on the whole course

1 Introduction

1 WHO IS THE COURSE FOR?

This course is designed for learners of English who, having achieved an advanced stage of competence in written English, feel the need for a structured programme of improvement in speaking it.

The need may be the result of various causes. Typically, earlier instruction will have concentrated heavily on reading and writing, perhaps because this has been the most efficient way of teaching in the large groups they have had to work in. Or the concentration may have been deliberate, reflecting a justified belief that many people are more likely to need to read and write English than to speak it extensively. Whatever the reason, many learners undoubtedly do find themselves in the position of having to take part in various kinds of spoken communication – very often in professional contexts – without the confidence that would enable them to do so comfortably.

Effective speaking, whether it takes place in a formal public setting or in a relaxed social context, involves more than pronunciation, of course. It is nevertheless in this area of proficiency that many learners tend to locate their problems. Their awareness of real, and sometimes imaginary, shortcomings, are inhibiting: they need a course which will remove some of the uncertainties they feel about how they perform when called upon to speak English.

2 THE NEED FOR CONFIDENCE

The importance of confidence building can scarcely be exaggerated. The course tries to be positive about pronunciation: it avoids presenting 'good pronunciation' as simply a matter of not making mistakes. Greater awareness of how the pronunciation system works is presented as an addition to the learner's resources, not as a collection of pitfalls to be avoided. It does not follow the perfectionist tradition, which demands native-speaker-like control of the sounds of a particular accent, and which regards everything else as an 'error'. Instead, users are encouraged to see pronunciation from the point of view of how it can best enable them to make their meanings and intentions clear to a listener.

The learners we have in mind will usually say, if asked, that their problems are of two kinds. There remain a number of English sounds – the vowels and consonants they have been working at for so long – that they have still not fully mastered. And there is a largely unexplored area of potential errors that they are likely to label 'intonation'. This course deals with both of these, and seeks to treat them as matters closely related both to each other and to the end of efficient communication which they serve.

Confidence building requires that we approach the two areas in different ways. Uneasiness about intonation arises largely because learners know little about it. Its reputation for difficulty and for slipperiness leads to its being neglected in most teaching programmes. There is nevertheless a widely-held, and often disabling, belief that it is 'very important': that failure to get it right can make one's speech unintelligible, offensive, laughable, and so on. The best way to remedy this worrying situation is to provide some insight into just how the intonation system really works, something that can be done without the enormous expenditure of time and effort that it is commonly believed to require.

Concern about particular sounds is tackled in a different way. Here one is covering ground that *will* have been covered before. Reducing anxiety consists largely, not in teaching something new, but in developing learners' powers of self-appraisal. It is helpful if they can be made aware, firstly of how much they are getting right, and secondly of the particular sounds they really do need to work on. If they then focus their attention upon the latter, the results will probably be more noticeable because they are working with a limited and clearly perceived objective in mind.

It remains to be said that there are advantages in working in the two areas simultaneously. Certain facts about the treatment of particular sounds can be more easily appreciated, and their execution more easily practised, if they are set in the context of a communicative utterance whose intonation we are able to take into account. This consideration, more than any other, has been responsible for the distinctive organisation of the course.

II The organisation of the course

3 INTONATION AND SEGMENTS

A special feature of this course is that students work on intonational matters in conjunction with segments (particular sounds). By bringing them together we can show their interdependence. We can also ensure that the work students do in one area supports and reinforces the work they do in the other.

The overall framework is, in fact, designed to give systematic treatment to **intonation**, since this is the area in which advanced learners are most likely to feel that they are deficient. The terms and categories used in the course to describe intonation are those of what has come to be known as the *Discourse* description. This is presented in detail in *The Communicative Value of Intonation in English*, Brazil, D. C., E.L.R., University of Birmingham, 1985. An outline of this description is provided in Section III below.

The developing intonational framework then provides a basis for isolating *potential problems with particular sounds* and for working on them in a communicative context.

The function of the **tone unit** is central to the work in both areas. The notion of speech as a step-by-step progress through the message the speaker wants to communicate, each step being prepared for mentally before being embarked upon, is fundamental to the course. An appreciation that speaking involves one in adding *tone unit to tone unit* as one proceeds, not, as one tends to think, word to word, is an important part of the awareness on which its successful use depends.

4 LISTENING FOR MEANING

All the units begin with some recorded material to which students are asked to listen as they would to a meaningful and interesting piece of communication: that is to say, in the way they would normally listen to something that they wanted to hear about. Students may need to listen more than once in some cases before proceeding to the activity that follows.

This activity is best carried out in pairs or small groups. Its purpose is to engage students in some kind of verbal interchange about what they have heard. This will ensure that they are thoroughly involved with the content, that is to say with *what* was being said, before they go on to attend to *how* it was said. You may find that other kinds of discussion will do this equally well. There are, however, two important reasons why some such preliminary activity should not be neglected.

One reason is that we do not normally attend consciously to the pronunciation of the language we hear or speak. It consequently requires considerable concentration to do so. It is better, therefore, if students are not compelled to do it at the same time as they are having to cope with the quite demanding business of putting together or responding to what is being said. It is better if they have recent working experience of the vocabulary and also of the grammatical organisation of the communicative event in question. The kind of task suggested is intended to give them a chance to make active use of as much of the language as possible and to be thoroughly at home with the content of that event, so that it has all become as 'automatic' as possible before they embark upon the much less natural business of listening for, and reproducing, particular sound patterns.

The other reason is the stress laid, throughout the course, on the way every aspect of pronunciation is related to the communicative context. The emphasis is not upon pronouncing words, or even sentences. It is rather upon speaking language *which is carrying a message*, and doing so in some situation in which that message matters to both speaker and listener. In this way it contrasts, for instance, with the practice of using lists of words to perfect the pronunciation of particular sounds. Some students may well want to focus upon the pronunciation of uncontextualised words – the 'citation forms' they find in dictionaries – but this course is designed to minimise that practice. The initial involvement in each unit with language as meaningful message – with matter that can be absorbed into one's own world of interest and talked about to others – is intended to start things off on the right foot.

5 LISTENING TO INTONATION

The opening recording of each unit is designed to provide a suitable context within which to focus upon the use of one feature of the intonation system. The 'Listening to intonation' tasks enable students to approach this feature in a number of ways: aural discrimination, imitation, prediction and free use of the feature are all involved in varying degrees. No attempt is made to incorporate a standard progression from one kind of activity to another, however, since the perception of what other speakers do, and the ability to do likewise oneself, are regarded as inseparable aspects of the same process of increasing awareness.

The approach is inductive. Students are encouraged wherever

possible to discover 'rules' and other regularities for themselves, and formulate them in their own terms, before these are stated in their institutionalised form. This is considered important as a general principle. It also seems to be the most suitable way of proceeding for students who are seeking such rules solely in order to be more in control of their own performance; that is, students who are unlikely to be interested in mastering a particular descriptive system for its own sake. One consequence of adopting the inductive approach is that, in the Student's Book, summaries of the content are held back until the end of each unit.

6 PAIRWORK

Pairwork and/or small groupwork is an important part of the suggested programme. The most obvious reason for this is that it is the best way of creating opportunities for the necessary practice, and particularly for practice in settings where students can regard themselves as being in either real or simulated interaction with someone else.

Practice apart, it is suggested that the various investigations, predictive exercises and problem-solving tasks that are prescribed from time to time should be done cooperatively. This is not just a way of helping students to clarify their understanding for themselves; it has the additional advantage that talk *about* the extracts and examples contained in the course is almost certain to involve quotation *from* them: students can therefore get invaluable experience of articulating the language they are quoting within the 'genuine' context of their own discussions.

7 INTONATION TRANSCRIPTS

The transcription conventions that are associated with the Discourse approach to intonation are introduced progressively throughout the course and the tasks require that students can both interpret and use these. This is seen as the best way of pinning down the otherwise elusive nature of intonation and so avoiding the vagueness that can so easily undermine one's confidence when working with it.

It is important, however, that when transcription tasks are set they do not have an effect that is the opposite of the desired one of confidence building. The 'model' transcripts given, both within the units and in the Answers, represent a version that has been agreed by a number of experienced transcribers. You, or your students (or both!), may sometimes disagree with them. Experience shows that when we are using recorded data it is not always possible, even for practised ears, to agree about what is happening. It is both honest and expedient to admit that there is sometimes room for doubt. If and when disagreement becomes an issue, it is best to represent it to students as a reason for reassurance: if the experts can't *always* agree, there is nothing to worry about if *they* can't! For them, transcription conventions are learning tools; and the attempt to transcribe is *first and foremost a learning activity*: there is no question of testing their ability to produce a perfectly accurate transcript.

8 LISTENING TO SOUNDS

While much of the content of Part 1 of each unit is likely to be new to most students, the use they need to make of Part 2 is far less predictable and likely to vary from student to student. The problems that advanced learners have in the pronunciation of segments are usually confined to a limited number of sounds which, for a variety of reasons they have always found – and continue to find – difficult. The design of Part 2 is intended to help them towards:

1 making an accurate diagnosis of these problems;
2 using the standard phonetic analyses that are available to find out what causes them.

The emphasis is upon making a *systematic examination of their own performance*.

Each unit provides material that can be used to discover exactly where difficulties lie. Tasks are set to ensure that students do actually *hear* the differences and similarities upon which the sound system of the language rests. Once problems have been identified, students are directed towards practice exercises which are appropriate to their individual needs.

The way in which Part 2 of each unit is used will depend to some extent upon whether the class is mono- or multilingual. If the former, problems are likely to be shared, and some of the more conspicuous problems can be dealt with in class teaching; if the latter, they may be different for every student. In either case, however, much of the work suggested can well be carried out outside class time, problems being brought back for teacher guidance at the next session. It might be expected that advanced learners will want to take responsibility for their own improvement in this way and to seek help only when it is needed.

Again, the purely negative implications of this kind of problem spotting should be avoided. For most students, the systematic recognition of how much they can already get right can remove a lot of the generalised anxiety under which they probably labour, and they should be encouraged to take this positive view of things.

9 PROMINENT SYLLABLES AND TARGET SOUNDS

The most obvious overlap between Parts 1 and 2 of the units resides in the attention given to **prominent syllables** in both of them. The significance of these for anyone who is pinpointing and practising particular segments is of considerable importance. The reasons for this are set out in Section IV below. It is sufficient if we say two things in anticipation here.

One is that the peculiar importance attaching to prominent syllables in any act of communication results in their being singled out for a special kind of emphasis. But a very similar kind of emphasis tends easily to get attached to *any syllable in which a particular segment is made the focus of attention*. Being concerned both with the placing of prominence *and* with the quality of a particular vowel or consonant can, therefore, pull the speaker in different – and frequently incompatible – directions. The problem is avoided if we *focus upon sounds when they occur in prominent syllables*. In this way, giving conscious attention to one aspect of pronunciation produces a result that is consistent with the requirements of the other.

The other point is that an approach that begins with prominent syllables enables us to give appropriate attention to the so-called 'reduced' vowels of English. The pronunciation of these vowels and its relationship with prominence is acknowledged to be one of the main sources of difficulty for foreign learners. Taking this way in enables us to see the matter in a new, and hopefully more helpful, light. In targeting sounds for special attention, we shall consistently have regard to whether they are in prominent syllables or not.

III The intonation system

10 THE DESCRIPTION

There is no generally agreed method of describing how the intonation system of English works. It is likely that some teachers who make use of this course will be familiar with a method which differs from the one used here. It is therefore necessary to provide an account of its main features. What is given here is no more than the kind of outline summary that teachers will need in order to guide users successfully through the units.

Descriptive categories and transcription conventions

11 THE TONE UNIT

The basic building block of speech is the **tone unit**. The beginnings and ends of tone units are marked by the symbol // :

// the bus stopped // we'd got to the terminus // and everyone got out //

12 PROMINENT SYLLABLES

Each tone unit of ordinary speech has either **one** or **two prominent syllables**. Prominent syllables are indicated by the use of upper-case letters:

// it was DARK // and DRIZZling a little //

// we were SOMEwhere in the coMMERcial district // but i WASn't sure WHERE //

13 TONE

The last prominent syllable in each tone is also a **tonic syllable**. The tonic syllable is the place at which a significant pitch movement or tone begins. There are five tones: **the falling, the rising, rise-fall, fall-rise** and **level**. The tonic syllable is underlined in transcripts and the tone is indicated by means of a small arrow placed at the beginning of the tone unit:

// ↘ and TURNed into an Alleyway // ↘ and STARted to WALK //

// ↗ LET me see if i've got it RIGHT //

// ↘↗ i CAN't remember anyone called MAry //

// → WELcome // → to our regular aTTENders //

(The rise-fall is not included in the course as it is not used much. The falling tone is nearly always a safer alternative.)

14 KEY

While each of the tones is realised by a different **pitch movement,** an entirely different set of meaningful choices is realised by **pitch level.** A meaningful pitch-level choice is made at each prominent syllable.

The pitch level of the first prominent syllable establishes the **key** of the tone unit. It may be **high, mid,** or **low.** High and low keys are indicated in this course by means of an upward or downward arrow, which is placed immediately before the relevant prominent syllable. Mid key is indicated by the absence of an arrow in this position.

// the <u>MO</u>tor car // re↑<u>DU</u>ces mobility //

// the OLD <u>LA</u>dy // was ↑ <u>SI</u>tting in the <u>PA</u>ssenger seat //

// she ASKED for the street she <u>WAN</u>ted // ↓ <u>MAR</u>ket street //

// the <u>SCO</u>rer // was <u>MAR</u>cos // the ↓ <u>SPA</u>nish <u>CAP</u>tain //

(The pitch level of the last prominent syllable in the tone unit determines the termination of the tone unit as high, mid or low. Termination is not treated in this course, but can be marked, if necessary, by means of an upward or downward arrow placed in front of the last prominent syllable. If there is only one prominent syllable, key and termination cannot be chosen independently.)

Recognising and imitating the intonation features

15 PROMINENCE

A starting observation can be that prominent syllables are 'highlighted' in some way, or made to be more 'noticeable' or 'sound more important'. It is not easy to go beyond this and say exactly what it is that we hear as prominence. Neither, therefore, is there an immediately simple way of telling learners what they should do when prominence is needed.

Complex changes of various kinds – changes in pitch, loudness, length and perhaps other features – all seem to be involved. Nor does it seem very helpful to focus upon a single syllable and ask whether, in any absolute sense, it can be said to be prominent or not: prominence is better regarded as something one can recognise only within the overall pattern of the tone unit of which it is part.

There is, however, a fairly easy way of getting a working understanding of the matter. Many words are given in their dictionary forms with a number of degrees of 'stress' marked. A common pattern is represented by the kind of word that has, besides a number of 'unstressed' syllables, a so-called 'secondary stress' towards the beginning and a 'primary stress' towards the end, e.g.:

'co²mmuni¹cation'.

Dictionary users are expected to know what is meant by this kind of notation without its being necessary to define 'stress', and it seems that most do, in fact, know. The physical nature of what is involved is actually just as complicated as that which enables us to perceive the two kinds of prominence. Indeed, it is exactly the same.

The stress pattern of such a word is no more nor less than the prominence pattern we give to that word when we speak it as a tone unit:

'co²mmuni¹cation' is the same thing as // coMMUniCAtion //.

Therefore:

1 secondary and primary stress are both equivalent to **prominence**;
2 primary stress additionally singles out its syllable as the **tonic syllable**.

We have seen that tone units do not necessarily have two prominent syllables: that is to say, a single syllable is designated both tonic syllable and sole prominent syllable. Correspondingly, many words have only primary stress, and here the same equivalence applies:

'no¹tation' is spoken as a tone unit as: // noTAtion //.

Helpful though this way of looking at the matter may be, it can encourage us to overlook one important fact. For the stress pattern given by the dictionary is intended to be thought of as a permanent property of the word. When we quote

'co²mmuni¹cation'

we always put the secondary and primary stresses in the same place. But there is no guarantee that these 'stressed' syllables will be prominent when the word is used in an act of communication and in conjunction with other words. Stress placement remains automatic only so long as words are cited rather than used. The allocation of prominence is not automatic: it is both variable and meaningful. The word/tone unit analogy is useful, therefore, only as a means of getting started. Further comparison between the two involves us in a consideration of, among other things, protected vowels. (See Notes 34 and 37 on protected vowels on pages 27 and 29.)

16 PROCLAIMING TONE

Unit 1 of the course is based on a sample of carefully scripted and well-rehearsed reading. The material is so contrived as to have **falling tones** in nearly (but not quite) all the tone units. This provides a pattern with which other tones can later be compared. It also coincides with what usually happens when we cite a word, as described above. When reading out a citation form from the dictionary, we actually have the option of using any of the tones, but in practice 'primary stress' is usually realised as prominence + falling tone. Falling tones can therefore be demonstrated and practised without going beyond what students can already recognise and do.

Students frequently complain that they 'can't hear' whether a pitch movement is rising or falling. In reality, they are probably confused about which part of the tone unit they are supposed to be listening to. Two potential causes of confusion can be anticipated in a discussion of falling tones:

1 The tonic syllable is the place at which the significant pitch movement begins, but it *continues to the end of the tone unit*. In the case of the falling tone, this means that after the initial fall the pitch stays low until a new tone unit begins. When there are several words after the tonic syllable it is necessary to guard against introducing further prominences.
2 The 'fall' that the description of the tone refers to can only occur if the movement begins high. This often requires *a step up to a suitable starting point*. If students focus upon this preparatory step up, instead of upon the subsequent glide down, they will probably want to call the tones that we call falling tones 'rising' tones. They have to appreciate that the fall we have in mind is one which occurs at a particular point in the overall pattern of the tone unit. This point is the prominence peak of the tonic syllable (see Fig. 1).

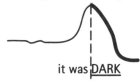

it was DARK

Fig. 1   Proclaiming tone

17 THE TONE SYMBOL

The use of terms like 'fall' and 'rise' probably overstresses the significance of vocal pitch in discriminating between different tones.

To make a working description of what happens in intonation we use its traditional definition as 'variation in the pitch of the voice', but a closer examination would reveal that variables other than pitch are involved, just as they are in the case of prominence. There is one practical consequence of this, and it affects the way we indicate tone choice in our transcriptions. The arrow ↘, which stands for proclaiming tone, is placed at the beginning of the tone unit, immediately after the boundary symbol, //. The reason for this is that, although we can be satisfied with 'falling' as a simplified description of one part of the tone unit, the tone one is aiming at does, in fact, affect everything one does. This includes what one does *before* the tonic syllable. Detailed attention to this would clearly be more burdensome than helpful, but it does mean that *speakers must address themselves to producing the tone unit as a whole*. They have to be aware from the outset of what tone is coming later: they can think in terms of necessary mental preparation for everything they will do before reaching it. There is a close similarity to a complex physical activity like serving in a game of tennis. The striking of the ball, like the production of a tonic syllable, is one event in a sequence of events, but it is unlikely to be successful if the preliminaries have not, in various ways, anticipated the strike. The placing of the arrow allows for this necessary anticipation and also serves as a reminder of the need for pre-planning.

18 REFERRING TONES

The two versions of the referring tone – the rising and the fall-rise – are introduced by comparing them with the falling. The most straightforward comparison we can make is between the falling and the rising, so this contrast is dealt with first. There is a possible problem here similar to the kind that was pointed out in connection with the falling. To rise, the speaker must begin low. This frequently requires a step down to the prominence peak of the tonic syllable before the rise that we focus upon begins (see Fig. 2). Students can, if not told otherwise, mistake rises for falls for this reason.

at the ¡TRAffic lights

Fig. 2   *Rising tone*

The step-up/step-down phenomenon is also useful in discriminating between the two referring tones, the rising and the fall-rise. Some students seem to have particular difficulty in distinguishing between these. The difficulty may well arise from the fact that the two tones have similar functions. When learners are using the tone system, not primarily as a matter of phonetic choice but as a means of making meaningful distinctions, the difference between them may easily get overlooked: substituting one for the other does not necessarily affect the implications of what one says in so obvious a way as would substituting a referring for a proclaiming tone or vice versa. If we need to establish the difference between the two by reference to phonetic shape alone, we can say that, while a fall-rise begins high, like a falling tone, a rising tone begins low: a clearly perceptible jump down to the starting point is often, therefore, the most obvious feature of the latter (see Fig. 3).

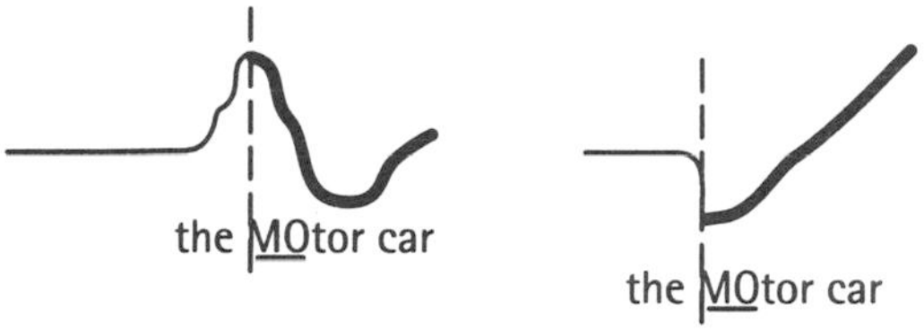

the MOtor car   the MOtor car

Fig. 3   Fall-rise tone   Rising tone

In recognising or producing a rising or a fall-rise tone we have to keep in mind that, here too, the meaningful pitch movement is distributed over all that part of the tone unit that begins with the tonic syllable. This means that, unless the tonic syllable is the last syllable in the tone unit, the 'end rise', which we have associated particularly with the 'referring' function, is not actually in the tonic syllable at all but near the end.

19 RECOGNISING KEY

The examples used to introduce the concept of key in Unit 8 have only one prominent syllable. This makes it possible to treat the pitch-level choice as a modification of the shape of the tone. Simply, the falling tone and the falling part of the fall-rise must begin at a particular level and this level can be raised or lowered with respect to what we might regard as the 'easiest' level for the speaker concerned to operate at (see Fig. 4).

Fig. 4   High, mid and low key with falling tones

There must be a particular pitch level which best suits the physical characteristics of each speaker, and students will readily appreciate that going above this level or below it makes great demands upon the speech mechanisms in much the same way as attempting to sing in the wrong register can. There is probably no need to do more than refer to the way in which we can usually tell when people are temporarily imposing such strains upon themselves to explain how high and low key are distinguished from a 'normal' mid key.

When key is determined at a tonic syllable which has a rising movement the relevant pitch level is that at which the rise ends (see Fig. 5).

Fig. 5   High, mid and low key with rising tones

When we introduce tone units with two prominent syllables, key is now determined by the pitch level at the earlier one, not the tonic. This enables us to make the general statement that it is always determined by the first prominent syllable. The pitch level concerned is now that of the first prominence peak (see Fig. 6).

// i STARted to WALK //

Fig. 6   A tone unit with two prominent syllables

It may be necessary to emphasise that it is the treatment of prominent syllables alone that affects the key of a tone unit. For instance, the level of any non-prominent syllables that come before the first prominent one is not significant.

20 RECOGNISING THE TONE UNIT

Both tone and key affect the meaning of the tone unit *as a whole*, not the meaning of the words of which it is composed. The tone unit is the smallest stretch of speech with which a particular choice of tone or key can be associated, and the least requirement for doing this is a tonic syllable. A stretch of speech has as many tone units as it has tonic syllables. Being aware of this, and following the message in the way the speaker intended it to be followed, does not necessarily require that listeners can tell where one tone unit ends and the next begins. Usually, we can tell they are distinct sections of the talk because of pauses or other discontinuities that separate them. The fact that the end of a tone unit provides an opportunity to take time to plan the next tends to increase the likelihood that boundaries will be distinctly audible in the speech of learners. If emphasis is placed upon having no break in continuity *within* the unit, the matter of what happens *between* units will very largely look after itself. It is best if students first grasp the concept of the 'whole tone unit' and understand the significance of the various meaningful intonation features that are associated with it. The fact that the end of one tone unit sometimes runs into the beginning of the next without there being a perceptible break can then be noted as something that does not alter the meaning.

The meaning of intonation

21 THE IMPORTANCE OF MEANING

Although it is obviously necessary to have a method of describing intonation features in terms of what they sound like, their real importance lies in the way they affect meaning. Intonation is not a 'tune' imposed arbitrarily upon speech: its use contributes to how speech carries a message. The goal to be aimed at is a situation in which students recognise and use the variations as *meaningful choices*. Even in a pronunciation course, therefore, meaning has to be the starting point.

A major source of difference among the ways intonation has been described has been disagreement about how its meaning can best be represented. Some have noted that a change in intonation seemingly alters the grammatical organisation of a sentence. Others have seen a relationship between the intonation of certain utterances and the supposed attitude or emotional state of the speaker. A problem with observations like these is that they seem only to apply on particular occasions. The task of pairing different kinds of utterance with different intonation patterns seems like an enormous, and perhaps even an open-ended, one. Having explained how intonation affects one sentence, you move on and find that a quite different kind of explanation is needed for the next.

The description used in this course seeks to provide an explanation which works for each and every occurrence of the feature in question. It will not, in general, be incompatible with explanations of other kinds, but will be concerned with principles of a more general kind than they are. This unavoidably requires that the meanings be stated in somewhat abstract terms. Some effort is required to get a working grasp of the way they operate. Against this can be counted the advantage that once a very small number of principles have been understood, they can be applied to everything one is likely to hear or likely to want to say. The system is finite and therefore learnable in its entirety.

22 SPEAKER–LISTENER UNDERSTANDING

To describe the meaning of any intonation feature, we have to think of the tone unit as being part of some interactive event: that is to say, the speaker is to be thought of as addressing a known listener, or listeners, at a particular moment in time. Each feature then reflects the speaker's view of what state of background understanding exists at that moment between speaker and listener. This means, of course, that discussion of the intonation of isolated sentences must be avoided: the context must always be taken into account.

23 SELECTION

When, as speaker, you assign a prominent syllable to a word, you indicate that this word represents a **selection**. The existing state of speaker–listener understanding determines whether each successive word **selects** one possibility from a number of them, or whether there is effectively no choice. The procedure can be seen at work in

// in the FIRST street on the <u>LEFT</u> //.

Here, the word 'left' occurs at a time in the narrative (in Unit 1) at which the alternative 'right' could easily have occurred; part of what the speaker needed to be told was that the required turning was on the one hand rather than on the other. Under these circumstances, one of the syllables of 'left' (and since it is a monosyllable that is the *only* one) is given prominence. A very similar argument applies to the other prominent syllable 'first'. But in a tone unit that comes later,

// and <u>TOOK</u> the left turning // (where she'd said)

'left' has no prominence. This is because by this time the likelihood of its being anything other than a left turning has been ruled out. What matters now is whether she took it or went straight past it, so 'took' is prominent. No relevant selection is made by 'turning' in either tone unit, something that is made evident by the fact that in some styles of conversation it could easily be missed out:

// in the FIRST on the <u>LEFT</u> //.

Yet another possibility enables us to take the notion of selection a step further:

// in the FIRST road on the <u>LEFT</u> //.

Clearly, there are cases where alternative words, like 'turning' and 'road' can occur and where the use of one rather than the other might be said to be the outcome of a process of 'selection'. But since *in this context* the choice makes no difference to the message – since for all practical purposes the two words are interchangeable – we can say that no **sense selection** is involved. And when this is the case no prominence is assigned.

In any discourse there are words which, at the moment they are spoken, *do* represent a sense selection and other words which *do not*. The way prominence is distributed reflects the speaker's view of how this two-way division of words is made. Another version,

// and took the <u>NEXT</u> turning //,

works, only if, as the speaker, you can rely upon your listener's prior understanding that taking the *next* turning rather than some other is now the only point at issue. It follows that the placing of prominent syllables can never be 'correct' in any generalisable sense; it can only be appropriate for the special conversational conditions in which the tone unit occurs.

24 PROCLAIMING AND REFERRING

The decision as to whether to **proclaim** or to **refer** is made on the basis of another kind of assessment of the present state of understanding. Essentially, it is a matter of whether speakers assume an *unshared perspective* or a *shared perspective* with regard to the content of the tone unit: whether they speak purely on their own behalf or whether they speak for both themselves and their listeners. It is easier to appreciate the implications of this if we first recognise another distinction: we need to know whether speakers are *telling* or *asking*.

25 TELLING SOMETHING

If the speaker is telling something, the content of a proclaimed tone unit contributes directly to what is told. This happens in

// ↘ you want the FIRST EXit // (p. 25 of the Student's Book)

Here, the speaker has information which the listener wants. The speaker draws upon his own, so far *unshared*, fund of knowledge in providing it.

In contrast, by producing another tone unit with a referring tone, either before or after the proclaimed tone unit, e.g.:

// ↗ when you come to the ROUNdabout // ↘ you want the FIRST EXit //

// ↘ you want the FIRST EXit // ↗ at the ROUNdabout //

a speaker can introduce a reference which does not further present business because it is already in play in the conversation. In this particular case the listener has already been told about the roundabout, so it can be said to be spoken from the viewpoint of both of them: it is not drawn from the speaker's private knowledge. Saying something with a referring tone does not result in a transfer of information: it goes back over ground that has already been negotiated and refers to what the speaker takes to be common ground.

Notice that a third version in which everything is proclaimed:

// ↘ you want the FIRST exit at the <u>ROUN</u>dabout //

does not assume that the roundabout has been mentioned previously.

Being able to mark the contents of successive tone units as already shared or not shared is useful in a variety of ways. In Unit 3, referring tones serve predominantly to mark shared recollections. The participants are together going over their memories of an earlier time when they worked together, and nothing new is told:

// ↘↗ there was the <u>POST</u> room // ↘↗ and then there was <u>AR</u>thur's

place // ↘↗ and there was the <u>PHO</u>tocopying room //

A common use is to fill in some qualification that a speaker assumes can be taken for granted.

(Where does this road lead to?)
// ↘↗ e<u>VEN</u>tually // ↘ it leads OUT onto the <u>BY</u>pass //

or

// ↘ it leads OUT onto the <u>BY</u>pass // ↗ e<u>VEN</u>tually //.

Doubtless it leads to many other places on the way; 'eventually', in both responses, means something like 'Although you don't actually say so, I take it you *mean* where will you get if you continue to the end'. Frequently the 'filling in' tone unit adds little to the message content:

// ↘↗ well <u>AC</u>tually // ↘ sub<u>SCRIP</u>tions will have to go <u>UP</u> //.

Here, the function of 'actually' can be described as an invocation of social togetherness. In itself, it doesn't make much difference to the import of the message, but the sense of shared understanding introduced by the referring tone helps things along by establishing a basis of general understanding. Often – as here – this softens the impact of a proclaimed assertion that will probably be unwelcome.

Comparatively clear-cut explanations of the uses of a particular tone like these can often be given by describing – or by imaginatively inventing – a familiar set of circumstances. They are very necessary, but in being specific it is important not to lose sight of what they all have in common. The point to emphasise is that the local effects can all be attributed to meaning difference that the proclaiming/referring distinction *always* makes.

26 ASKING

If speakers are asking, the distinction operates in a slightly different way. A proclaimed tone unit now indicates that matter available to the listener is not yet available to the speaker. The sought-for transfer of information comes about as a result of the listener replying appropriately:

// ↘ perHAPs i could go by aNOther route // (Unit 4, p. 42 of the Student's Book).

By using referring tones, speakers proceed *as though the requisite information were available to them also*, but ask the listener to confirm that what they are assuming to be true is, indeed, true:

// ↗ is THAT the TITle // (Unit 4, Conversation 1)

The assistant assumes that the customer has enquired about the book by its title (people usually *do*!) but wants to check before going any further. If the purpose of a proclaimed enquiry is to *find out*, then that of one with a referring tone is to *make sure*.

There are two kinds of problem that might be encountered in applying this simple account. One arises from the fact that people often use 'making sure' questions where 'finding out' questions might seem to be a better representation of the true situation. There is often no way of knowing whether someone genuinely has prior expectations about the answer or whether they are totally in the dark. This means that they can behave as if they had a hunch and exploit the implied togetherness for social ends. This frequently happens in phatic enquiries, where the actual transfer of information is known by both parties to be of only secondary importance. Such a friendly opener as

// ↗ ARE you enJOying the course //

can be compared with a real attempt to get reactions like

// ↘ do you HAVE any CRIticisms to offer //.

The other problem is the expectation many have that *wh-* questions will have falling intonation and *yes/no* questions will have rising intonation. The partial truth on which this frequently heard assertion rests is no more than a tendency. Probably we are more likely to be finding out when we use a question with a *wh-* word, and more likely to be making sure when we use a *yes/no* question. We should be clear, though, that both kinds of tone are used with both 'types' of question; and the reasons for using either exactly parallel the reasons that apply in 'telling' situations. More importantly, perhaps, there are many occasions when asking does not involve the use of an utterance that one can recognise as a 'question' of either type. The rules regarding intonation apply to these as well.

27 WHO IS IN CHARGE?

To explain the use of the two versions of referring tone, the fall-rise and the rising tone, we need to make use of the notion of **dominance**. The dominant participant is the one who, for the time being, is in control of the conversation or other verbal event. In some events, like the chairperson's speech in Unit 5, one person is put in control by some kind of institutionalised procedure. At the other extreme, some kinds of social conversation frequently see many changes in the balance, as participants compete with each other for control.

Learners are likely to have had little experience of negotiating this kind of role change in English. In their capacity as *students* they will have acted almost exclusively as non-dominant speakers. They are also unlikely to have had practice in using the dominant rising tone that they may need if they are to be effective in 'public' contexts. For these reasons, sensitisation to what is involved seems to be important.

It has to be recognised, however, that rather complex cultural practices often determine when it is appropriate to assume dominance and when it is not. Sometimes the effect of changing from one to the other is scarcely noticeable. In view of this, it seems best to give students the chance to get the feel of using one tone or the other in situations where the effect is clearly noticeable and where one choice or the other can be said to be significantly preferable. Unit 6 does this by concentrating on utterances where the question 'Who stands to benefit?' is a real issue.

The proposition that when the speaker is seeking to help someone it is often appropriate to be 'forceful', but when seeking help for oneself it is often better not to be, places the matter in the context of fairly well-recognised expectations about human behaviour.

28 THE MEANING OF KEY

Choice of key for any tone unit depends, as do the other choices, upon assumptions one makes about the listener's present view of things. **High key** attributes certain expectations to the listener and contradicts them. High key therefore has *contrastive* implications: 'not X (as one might expect) but Y'. The use of **low key**, on the other hand, attributes expectations and confirms them: 'X (which you would naturally expect after Y)'. **Mid key** can then be said to attribute no expectation of this kind.

In all this, it has to be kept in mind, however, that to attribute an expectation conversationally, you do not necessarily have to believe your listener is really entertaining it. You can contradict a belief just in case they do! In Unit 8, someone interviewed on the subject of transport sets out to refute a lot of what he takes to be commonly held views about the advantages of private cars. Much of what he says would probably accord with, rather than contradict, what the interviewer and many of the listeners would say. It is common practice, however, to make a case by setting up an imaginary upholder of the opposite case to argue with.

The same interview also illustrates the way high key can often seem to be indicating an 'emotional' response or a certain 'attitude'. It is easy to show that no label we might put on the attitude could be correctly attributed to the key choice. If this speaker is 'disapproving', 'angry', 'indignant' or 'critical', very similar intonation would indicate the opposite feelings if used by someone who was enthusiastically arguing for, for instance, faster cars and more multi-storey car parks to put them in.

29 ORIENTATION TOWARDS YOUR LISTENER OR YOUR LANGUAGE?

The appropriate use of each of the features we have mentioned above requires that the speaker is *directly orientated* towards a hearer. This means that there is an addressee who both shares a certain amount of the speaker's background and can be assumed to have a present interest in the 'message' that the speaker is seeking to convey.

Some speech events, however, like some kinds of 'reading out' and the carrying out of certain ritualised procedures, amount to no more than the vocalising of *what is written*, or *what is habitually said*. This is to say that no assumptions at all are made about a listener. Speech which occurs in these circumstances is *obliquely orientated*: the speakers can be thought of as being engaged with the language purely *as language*. We can say that they are thinking about what they are saying rather than about what message they are trying to convey.

Oblique discourse makes use of proclaiming tones in the special sense of 'I tell you what is written here', or 'I tell you what it is customary to tell you on occasions like this'. It also makes use of the special **level tone** or o-tone.

As well as occurring in pre-coded discourse, level tone often occurs at points of hesitation. Speakers often hesitate because they are having some kind of difficulty in putting together the language the present situation demands. In these circumstances, there is a temporary shift of attention from the listener (direct orientation) towards the language (oblique orientation). The effect of such a shift can often be interpreted as something like 'Wait a moment while I work out what to say next'. Not surprisingly, this kind of orientation shift is common in the speech of people – whether learners of the language or native speakers – who are having to think before they speak.

It is evident that we do not need actually to teach learners to hesitate! Neither do we need to teach the use of the level tone that often precedes hesitation. It seems important, however, that both students and teachers should be aware of its function. One reason why the intonation of much naturally-occurring speech is far less tidy than the tasks in this course might lead one to expect is that level tones can occur almost anywhere, and for no other reason than that the speaker needs to divert his or her attention to the business of putting the language together. Another reason is that, although the belief on which much of this course is founded is that we can expect learners to use intonation in a purposeful and helpful way, it would be unreasonable to expect them to display a level of 'fluency' which exceeds that which native speakers can usually manage. We must expect involuntary uses of level tone often to break up those patterns that are fully exemplified only when attention can be given entirely to satisfying a listener's present needs.

IV Identifying sounds for attention

30 SOUNDS AND SYMBOLS

If appropriate phonetic symbols are used it is possible to represent each of the successive 'segments' of any stretch of speech separately. Thus

// i WALKed aLONG // LOOking at the WINdows //

might be represented as

/ aɪ wɔːkt əlɒŋ lʊkɪŋ ət ðə wɪndəʊz /.

The aim of this course, however, is not to provide this kind of total coverage. To give meticulous and detailed attention to each of the 24 segments would certainly be beyond the capacity of any learner. Advanced students need a procedure for identifying particular sounds so that they can examine, and if necessary modify, their performance of them, one at a time, and without being unduly diverted from whatever act of communication they are involved in. They need to recognise, moreover, that meticulous and detailed attention is neither necessary nor desirable in every case. Part 2 of each unit has been designed with these considerations in mind.

31 SOUNDS IN PROMINENT SYLLABLES

An essential feature is the significance of **prominence**. In the tone unit

// we'd GOT to the TERminus //

the syllables 'GOT' and 'TER-' demand special attention from the listener because, as we have said, they distinguish their words as representing significant selections. It is reasonable to suggest that the speaker's attention should be focussed there, too. We therefore have a reason for beginning the business of 'listening to sounds' by concentrating upon vowels and consonants that occur in such syllables. For instance, when the focus is upon vowels, those of 'GOT' and 'TER-', /ɒ/ and /ɛː/, will first be given attention.

It is possible to find tone units in which all the simple vowels of English except /ə/ and all the diphthongs occur in prominent syllables. Since, however, all words can, in particular circumstances, occur without prominence, it is also possible to find the same vowels and diphthongs in non-prominent syllables as well. For example, the vowel /ɒ/ occurs in a non-prominent syllable in

// EVeryone got OUT //.

Students are not, however, encouraged to focus upon /ɒ/ here. Every advanced student will have a working approximation to every English sound. They can, provisionally at least, be satisfied with this in non-prominent positions.

There are two reasons for adopting this approach. One is that a deviant sound will be less noticeable and less disruptive of effective communication in a non-prominent syllable than in prominent ones. The other is that all correction is a matter of making choices. The speaker is effectively in the position of having to choose between a sound that is judged to be the proper one for the occasion and the 'non-English' one that is being rejected. This means that the process is very similar to that which results in a prominent syllable being assigned to a word: selecting one sound rather than another is much like selecting one word rather than another. The result is often that the syllable concerned is given prominence inappropriately. If the precise pronunciation of /ɒ/ is foregrounded in the above example, the result is likely to be

// EVeryone <u>GOT</u> // <u>OUT</u> //.

It is likely that the obtrusive and communicatively unjustified prominence in 'GOT' will be more of a problem to the listener than a slightly un-English vowel would have been.

To help with identifying some sounds for attention in the early units, tasks centre upon what happens at a number of **target positions** in the tone unit. These have the effect of directing attention to the sounds *in and around the prominent syllables*. The target positions are as follows:

1 Vowels in prominent syllables
2 Consonants and consonant clusters at the beginning of prominent syllables
3 Vowels, consonants and consonant clusters at the end of prominent syllables which are also at the end of the tone unit
4 Consonants and consonant clusters that follow the vowel of a prominent syllable but do not end the tone unit.

Initially, single sounds – simple vowels, diphthongs and consonants – are examined in each of these positions, a procedure which enables students to build up their own inventory and, very importantly, to *identify their own problems*. Awareness exercises enable them to appreciate what is meant by the distinctions **voiced/unvoiced**, **plosive/fricative**, **long/short**, and to examine how far their particular problems arise from failure to make such distinctions. The phonetic analysis goes only so far as seems likely to be helpful in pursuing this limited aim. One consequence of this is that consonants that phonologists assign to three different classes – **nasals**, **laterals** and **approximants** – are referred to collectively as **NLA** sounds.

The so-called 'consonant clusters' are then examined in Target Positions 2 and 3. A different treatment is given to sequences of consonants that come *within the tone unit*. What is central here is the question of the extent of prominence. If we take the vowel of each prominent syllable as a starting point, then:

– if a single consonant follows it sounds as if it belongs to the following (usually non-prominent) syllable;
– if there are two or more consonants following, the first sounds as though it belongs to the prominent syllable, and any remaining consonants sound as though they belong to the next syllable.

This applies even in the case of sequences of consonants that would be regarded as 'clusters' elsewhere.

This procedure often results in a division into 'syllables' which differs from that which standard phonological criteria would give. It is not suggested that it will necessarily cover all cases. It is adopted simply to provide an easy way for students to get a feel of the principles of English syllabification.

32 PROTECTED VOWELS

Another reason for concentrating on the vowels of prominent syllables is that it enables us to recognise a class of sounds which we refer to as **protected vowels,** that is to say, those vowels which have a more or less constant value wherever they occur. The special feature of protected vowels is as follows. For any particular speaker, their sounds can be specified within fairly narrow limits. The sounds in the prominent syllables of

// we'd GOT to the TERminus // and EVeryone got <u>OUT</u> //

do not vary much between one performance and the next. The same cannot be said, however, of any of the remaining vowels. In

// we'd GOT to the TERminus //

the five remaining vowels are **unprotected.** It is often said that these are 'reduced' to /ə/ or to the weak form of /ɪ/, so that the whole tone unit sounds something like this:

/ wɪd ɡɒt tə ðə tɜːmɪnəs /.

Although this transcription represents a fairly predictable way of pronouncing the tone unit, it does not represent the whole truth. There are, in fact, a range of possible pronunciations for many unprotected vowels. Either /iː/ or /ɪ/ could be used in 'we'd' and either /ʌ/ or /ə/ in the last syllable of 'terminus' without the speaker departing from perfectly acceptable English practice. Much depends upon how careful the speaker is being at the time and how quickly he or she is speaking.

In the case of the unprotected vowels, natural-sounding speech results, not from the speaker taking careful and accurate aim at a particular sound, but from a recognition that there is a range of possibilities and it is not very important which one is chosen. Sounds like /ə/ and /ɪ/, which are often used, result from speakers adopting a relaxed and 'permissive' attitude towards their pronunciation rather than taking the care that is appropriate for protected vowels.

It is not always possible, in a limited corpus, to find tone units in which all the protected vowels are located in prominent syllables. The

/ɒ/ in 'got' in

// EVeryone got <u>OUT</u> //

is protected, although the syllable is non-prominent. By working mainly with tone units in which protection and prominence coincide, it is possible to encourage the desired 'neglect' of unprotected vowels by giving *somewhat exaggerated attention to protected ones.*

33 WHICH WORDS HAVE PROTECTED SYLLABLES?

This question is best answered by considering monosyllabic and polysyllabic words separately.

1 All words of more than one syllable have at least one protected vowel. Some have two.
2 The vowel of a monosyllable is protected if it is a content word but not if it is a function word.

34 WHICH VOWELS OF A PARTICULAR WORD ARE PROTECTED?

This question arises only in the case of polysyllabic words. The citation form of such words provides the answer. When spoken in isolation – that is to say, as complete tone units – the words

// co<u>MMER</u>cial //   // po<u>LICE</u> //   // <u>TER</u>minus //   // <u>STA</u>tion //

have protected vowels as marked

   comm|er|cial   pol|i|ce   t|er|minus   st|a|tion

If the citation form of a word has two prominent syllables, then the vowels in both are protected:

// MANu<u>FAC</u>ture //   // enVIronMENtally //

   m|a|nuf|a|cture   env|i|ronm|e|ntally.

   Notice that when any of these words is used in a situation where it does not represent a significant selection, and where it would therefore be inappropriate for it to be given a prominent syllable, the vowel nevertheless retains its 'full' sound:

// the <u>BUS</u> t|er|minus //   // the po<u>LICE</u> st|a|tion //.

35 VARIATION IN UNPROTECTED VOWELS

The amount of noticeable variation in the sound of unprotected
vowels is different from one vowel to another. The first vowel of
'police', often described as /ə/, might have anything between the 'full'
sound /ɒ/ and practically no sound at all. There are some cases,
however, where the variation is very slight, a fact which somewhat
obscures the simple pattern we have described.

One instance is found in the words whose citation forms are

// <u>DIS</u>trict //   and   // re<u>STRICT</u> //.

The first of these has a protected vowel in the first syllable and the
second has one in the second syllable. The fact that, in both cases, the
first and second vowel sounds are very similar is due, of course, to
there being little difference between the 'negligent' pronunciation of
the vowel /ɪ/ in the non-prominent syllable of each and the carefully
targeted pronunciation of the same vowel in the prominent one. Both
are customarily represented by the same symbol. There is, in fact, a
phonetic difference between them, describable largely in terms of
length, but in order to recognise it we should need to embark on more
detailed description than would be likely to be helpful to learners.

Much the same is true of the 'full' and 'reduced' forms of the
diphthongs, something that is made the subject of Task 7.12. The
pronouns *he* and *I* are both single-syllable function words and
therefore have unprotected vowels. But while the vowel of *he* shows
the variation we should expect (it is often closer to /ɪ/ than /iː/, *I* never
moves far enough from the 'full' diphthong /aɪ/ to justify using any
other symbol. It is tempting to say that all diphthongs are protected,
but to do so would be to overlook the fact that they *are* variable, albeit
within fairly narrow limits. The important point is that they should
not be targeted except when they occur in prominent syllables.

36 FULL FORMS OF UNPROTECTED VOWELS

The pronunciation given to an unprotected vowel depends upon,
among other things, the circumstances in which it occurs. There are
three circumstances in which it varies little, if at all, from the 'full'
sound:

1 when it is followed immediately by another vowel
   // it's on th[e] Other <u>SIDE</u> //;
2 in some cases when a monosyllable comes at the end of a tone unit
   // i'll COME if i C[A]N //;

3 always when the syllable is made prominent
// i said termiN[U]S // not termiNAL //
// she DIDn't know where she W[A]S //.

37 PROTECTED VOWELS IN NON-PROMINENT SYLLABLES

In Unit 5 students are encouraged to 'neglect' all sounds that do not
occur in prominent syllables. Then Unit 7 presents them with the
rather more difficult objective of giving full value to protected vowels
without inadvertently giving them prominence. An example would be

// EVeryone got OUT //

where the vowel of 'got' has its 'full' value, but must nevertheless *not*
be targeted.

38 REDUCED VOWELS

The procedure, therefore, requires students to give attention, firstly to
the sounds of prominent syllables, then to protected vowels in non-
prominent syllables. The only sounds that are not given attention are
the reduced sounds, and particularly /ə/. This may seem surprising,
given that it seems often to be an inability to produce these sounds in
the proper places that marks a learner's pronunciation as 'non-
English'.

In this, as in so many matters, it is important to keep in mind the
learner's state of competence. Many absolute beginners doubtless need
to be told about /ə/ and to practise it. This leads to its being included
among the inventory of sounds, alongside the other vowels. It leads
also, in effect, to its being targeted: learners are told to say /pəliːs/ and
not /pɒliːs/. The resulting situation is not one which suits the rather
different needs of the advanced learner. We have said that, in natural-
sounding speech, the peculiar quality of /ə/ arises precisely from its *not*
being targeted: it sounds the way it does because the speaker has no
clearly-defined vowel in mind. The appropriate attitude is one which
accommodates an alternation between what we might call 'care' and
'neglect'. This course seeks to engender and constantly reinforce such
an attitude by drawing students' attention to everything *except* the
neglectable sounds.

39 RHYTHMICITY

This same alternation of attention and inattention contributes to a
particular kind of rhythmicity which is often said to be an important

feature of spoken English. 'Stress timing', as this feature is often called, is said to be the result of a tendency for 'stressed' syllables to occur at roughly similar time intervals. No explicit mention is made in the course of this tendency. Certain rhythmic implications do, however, attach to many of the tasks.

If 'prominence' is substituted for 'stress' in the way the effect is described, then it is possible to perceive a tendency for all two-prominence tone units to be spoken with nearly the same time interval between the prominences. In tone units like

// we'd GOT to the   TERminus //
 // EVeryone got   OUT //
 // she WENT down a narrow Alleyway //

there is a perceptible speeding up of the medial non-prominent syllables (including the one with a protected vowel in 'narrow') when more syllables have to be included between the prominent ones.

Much of the material for repetition in the course comprises variations on the two-prominence pattern. In practice, this will probably strengthen the tendency to observe this kind of rhythmicity. 'Stress timing' over longer stretches of speech can, of course, be practised separately and mechanically. The reasons for not doing so in a course for advanced learners are as follows.

It is possible to say:

// the BUS STOPPED // we'd GOT to the TERminus // and EVeryone got OUT //

in such a way that there seem to be approximately equal time intervals between all consecutive prominent syllables:

BUS	STOPPED	GOT	TER	EV	OUT.

Even when this is not the case, it may be that some automatic tendency towards regular timing results in some pauses *between* tone units being approximately equal to the time lapses *within* tone units. So 'silent stresses' might be perceived thus:

BUS	STOPPED	^	GOT	TER	^	EV	OUT.

This is the kind of performance that results from the use of nursery rhymes and jingles in elementary language classrooms. But for a speaker actually to produce such a regular 'beat', it is necessary for the entire sequence of tone units to be mentally available, either as a written text or as memorised material, before the performance begins.

It assumes that the speech is in some way pre-rehearsed. Attention is frequently drawn in this course to the usefulness of tone unit boundaries as a point at which any necessary new planning can take place. The view we take of the learner is of someone who is having to put together the language as they go along. Clearly, the planning of this extract as three separate parcels will make lighter demands upon the speaker than would putting it together as a whole before speaking begins.

Learners are likely, in general, to need more frequent and perhaps longer periods of 'planning time' than native speakers, and it is scarcely realistic to think that they can be concerned with rhythmic considerations at the same time as they are occupied with assembling the next bit of the discourse. By drawing attention to rhythm solely in relation to what happens *within* the tone unit, we can recognise the speaker's frequent need to grapple with language problems *between* tone units. If there is, indeed, a generalised tendency to speak rhythmically over longer stretches, then the ability to do this can be safely assumed to come with increased confidence and fluency. It is more conducive to confidence building in learners to hand over the time between tone units to them: to encourage them to make whatever planning use of it they find necessary and take as much or as little time over it as they need.

Part 2: Notes on the units

Unit 1 Step by step

This unit has two main aims: to introduce the idea of the **tone unit** as the basic pronunciation building block; and to make students consciously aware of how **prominent syllables** can be recognised within a tone unit. These features are made the basis of everything that comes later in the course. Note that this applies whether attention is being directed specifically towards intonation matters or towards the pronunciation of segments. It is therefore important that enough time be given to the tasks in this unit to ensure that tone units and prominent syllables can be identified with reasonable confidence, and that students appreciate what it means, both to the speaker and to the listener, to progress *tone unit by tone unit* rather than word by word.

Summary

(Note: Since students are encouraged to adopt an exploratory approach to the material, the Student's Book has summaries at the end of each unit. Teachers will probably find that having them at the beginning will be more convenient.)

1 Instead of thinking of speech as a sequence of 'words' – as we are inclined to do when examining the written language – we can think of it as a sequence of **tone units**.
2 Each tone unit is a separate parcel of information which we present to the listener, and the way we arrange information in parcels is important if we are to be readily understood.
3 Each tone unit has either one or two **prominent syllables**, and prominent syllables are placed in such a way as to draw the listener's attention to particular words.
4 When you find it necessary to practise particular sounds, it is better to begin by targeting those that come in prominent syllables. All the simple vowels except /ə/ and the diphthongs can be found in prominent syllables.

Listening for meaning

Students should be discouraged from trying to remember the exact *language* of the original. By focussing upon the sequence of *events* they have just heard about, they will have preparatory experience of putting together a message in their own way; and by doing it with a partner as recipient, they will appreciate that what they are doing involves both a speaker and a listener. Both of these considerations are important for the way spoken communication is treated in this course.

Listening to intonation

1.1

In the material used in this task, and in most others in Unit 1, tone unit boundaries usually coincide with very clear pauses. It may simplify matters at this stage simply to rely on pauses to determine where tone units begin and end. There is no harm in this, provided it is seen as no more than a provisional expedient.

Students may also notice that the tone units included in this task coincide with major grammatical chunks, which are often sentence-like. Attention can be directed in subsequent activities to the fact that there is no reliable relationship between tone units on the one hand and 'sentences' or 'clauses' or any other kind of grammatical item on the other.

If this task is done in pairs, there is likely to be a great deal of informal repetition of the material, and students will consequently become more at home, both in handling it and in perceiving tone units.

Something to be stressed is that, while the length of pause can vary, allowing the speaker or reader just as much time as is needed to 'prepare' for the coming tone unit, the tone unit itself must be spoken as an uninterrupted whole.

The notion of speech as a step-by-step progress through the message the speaker wants to communicate, each step being 'prepared' mentally before it is embarked on, is crucial to what comes later in the course, and could usefully be discussed at this early stage.

ANSWERS

2 but it was too late // they'd gone // the street was empty // even the bus driver had gone/

3 I hurried across // and turned into an alleyway // and started to walk //
4 it was one of those pedestrian precincts // no cars admitted // with concrete benches // to sit on // and concrete tubs // for plants //

1.2

This task follows a pattern that is often repeated throughout the course: students are asked to listen to examples, and then to 'get the feel' of repeating them, *before they are discussed in analytical terms.*

The placing of the prominent syllables in these items should raise few problems. Students are given only a very brief working description of what 'prominence' is at this stage. The matter is returned to in Unit 7. It is better to introduce the notion through examples than through phonetic description. (See Note 15 on prominence on pages 9–10.)

Some students have problems with tone units that continue for more than a syllable or so after the tonic syllable. The way they cope with // where MARket street was // might give warning of such a problem. The thing to emphasise is that there should be no more prominent syllables after the tonic syllable.

1.3

Once more, avoid trying to 'define' prominence. It is enough that students can hear where it occurs.

1.4

This task is designed principally to familiarise students with the transcription conventions that have been introduced up to this point:

// = tone unit boundary

UPPER-CASE LETTERS = both kinds of prominent syllable.

The practice of underlining tonic syllables is introduced after the completion of the task.

It may be necessary to point out that normal punctuation is not used when transcribing intonation, and upper-case letters do not have their usual function. (Notice, for instance, that the pronoun 'I' is not capitalised.) In some informal writing commas, question marks, underlinings and such like are often used to suggest intonation, but they do not represent it in any consistent way, and are therefore not useful for present purposes.

If students lack confidence in tackling this task, it may be better to proceed one tone unit at a time, giving plenty of time to read and make mental preparation of, for instance,

// but the BENches were <u>WET</u> //

before attempting to say it. If this piecemeal approach is adopted, a second stage should be to attempt the complete sequence of tone units:

// but the BENches were <u>WET</u> // it was <u>WIN</u>ter // and there WASn't a <u>PLANT</u> // to be <u>SEEN</u> //

before going on to a similar two-stage treatment of the next piece.

1.5

If sufficient cassette-recorders or language laboratory facilities are available, this should be done in small groups. Even if you have neither of these, students should be encouraged to say what they think they are hearing: that is to say, to repeat the tone unit in the same way as it is spoken in the recording. It is important that both teacher and students see this activity as giving 'hands-on' experience of describing intonation. The fact that some people make different judgments about what they hear must not be allowed to undermine confidence at this early stage.

Differences are most likely to be of two kinds:

1 Tone units will be thought to include either one or two prominent syllables, e.g.:

// <u>HO</u>lly // and <u>SNOW</u>men //   or
// HOlly and <u>SNOW</u>men //.

2 Different words may be given a prominent syllable within a tone unit, e.g.:

// in the FIRST street on the <u>LEFT</u> //   or
// in the FIRST <u>STREE</u>t on the left //.

The significance of doing either of these two things might be discussed informally at this stage. It is examined in the next three tasks.

ANSWERS

1 // i passed some shops // brigh lights // and bargains // and fashionable dresses // on plastic figures // videos // and fridges // and

(hundreds of(shoes)// at (give)away (pri)ces // (left)over(gift) wrapping //
and (ho)lly // and (snow)men //

2 // she(thought)there was a(pub)// in the(first)street on the(left)//
pe(rhaps)they'd know(there)//

3 // there was just(no)body a(bout) // i (walked) (on)// and(took)the left
(tur)ning // (where)she'd(said)// and(found)the pub //

(See the comment on the accuracy of transcriptions in Note 7 on
pages 5–6.)

1.6

This task is designed to show the difference between a single, two-
prominence tone unit, and two, one-prominence tone units, when
falling tones occur throughout. It is quite likely that failure to
appreciate the difference will have arisen in the course of Task 1.5.

It should be pointed out that neither version is more 'correct' than
the other: there are times when it is better to present a certain amount
of information as 'one parcel' and times when it is better to present it
as two. For instance, we may want to draw separate attention to the
fact that there were different articles in the window – // VIdeos // and
FRIdges // – or we may only want to have them all thought about as
electrical appliances – // VIdeos and FRIdges //.

Some students may suggest that the parcelling of information has
something to do with grammar (see Note 21 on pages 15–16). Though
this idea should not be rejected out of hand, it is better not to pursue
it. What is often needed is the confidence to produce the two-
prominence tone unit when one wants to; it is easy to see that the
longer single tone unit requires more 'advance planning' than does a
two-tone unit version. For instance, to begin

// VIdeos // (*pause*) and FRIdges //

you need only to be sure of the way ahead as far as the end of 'videos';
but before you begin

// VIdeos and FRIdges //

you need to have cleared up any planning problems you may have as
far as the end of 'fridges'.

ANSWERS

4 // <u>HO</u>lly // and <u>SNOW</u>men //

   // <u>HO</u>lly and <u>SNOW</u>men //

5 // there WASn't a <u>PLANT</u> // to be <u>SEEN</u> //

   // there WASn't a plant to be <u>SEEN</u> //

6 // i WALKed a<u>LONG</u> // <u>LOO</u>king at the <u>WIN</u>dows //

   // i WALKed along looking at the <u>WIN</u>dows //

1.7

Informal discussion of // where <u>MAR</u>ket street was // is intended to provide some starting points for the longer exploratory work in Task 1.8. It is fairly easy to see that if the shop assistant failed to hear 'street' she would still probably know what Elizabeth was looking for. If she didn't hear 'market' she probably wouldn't know. Apart from the general purpose of 'helping your listener to follow your message', no attempt need be made at this stage to give a formal answer to the question the rubric poses.

1.8

This task is included here to help students appreciate that the proper placing of prominences is not a mechanical matter: *it amounts to a deliberate highlighting of certain parts of the message* and the decision as to which parts need to be highlighted depends upon *the special circumstances of the moment.*

The examples chosen are intended to allow students to find their own way of stating the significance of assigning, or *not* assigning, a prominent syllable to a word. There are, therefore, no 'correct' answers here. Ideas that would suggest that they were thinking on the right lines might be:

1 The fact that it was a 'holiday' job, rather than a 'regular' job has an obvious bearing upon how much the assistant knows about the town.
2 She only 'thought' there was a pub, she didn't claim to 'know'.
3 'Left', as opposed to 'right', is crucial to the message.
4 Elizabeth could have decided to walk 'back'; instead she walked 'on'. She wasn't going to give up yet!

5 The time the pub opened is stated as 'seven'; if it had been 'six', she might have thought it was worth waiting.

6 The verb 'do' is the only one that is likely to be used in connection with 'a job'.

7 In the context, some word meaning 'the district' is fairly predictable. (Of course, she could have said // she didn't <u>KNOW</u> the area //, but then 'area' – or another possibility, 'neighbourhood' – would have meant the same thing as 'district'.)

8 In 'Perhaps they'd know there', it can be taken for granted that Elizabeth is looking for somewhere where they will 'know'. Is there any other verb that could have been used instead?

9 In 'and took the left turning, where she'd said' there is now no real possibility of it being anything but 'left'. Why?

10 In 'the first street on the left' there is no alternative to 'on', so it does not need special attention. (Compare this with (4).)

When pairs have found ways of expressing their own reasons, they can be asked to report back to the class, so that their explanations can be compared with others'. They should be encouraged to mention the example they are explaining *with the original intonation* in the course of their explanations.

1.9

The version on the cassette is as follows:

// there was NO <u>AN</u>swer // i RANG a<u>GAIN</u> // it was GEtting <u>COLD</u> //

so i deCIded to go <u>BACK</u> // i <u>SHOU</u>ld have come // in the <u>DAY</u>time //

THIS was <u>HOPE</u>less // i could be WAlking a<u>BOUT</u> // ALL <u>NIGHT</u> //

and <u>NE</u>ver find market street // i WENT <u>BACK</u> // to where the <u>SHOPS</u>

were // it was <u>RAI</u>ning // <u>HARD</u> // and the <u>PRE</u>cinct // was de<u>SER</u>ted //

i felt <u>VE</u>ry // <u>MIS</u>erable //

The reason for making the comparison is simply to give experience of hearing – and recognising – what different versions sound like. Though students may readily see that some are more likely than others, the question of which are 'correct' should be avoided: the exact way information is packaged depends very much upon circumstances.

If students notice that some of the tonic syllables, both in their own versions and in the recorded one, have pitch movements that do not fall, this observation can be noted and referred back to in Unit 2.

Listening to sounds

1.10

This task, like some others that are included in the 'Listening to sounds' sections of the early units, is intended to get students thinking about similarities and differences. The question is whether two sounds count as the 'same' sound when they are used in English or whether they count as different sounds. Working through tasks like this will give them an opportunity to clarify the issue for themselves in particular cases.

The idea of pinpointing target positions within tone units will probably be new to students and may need further discussion.

ANSWERS

1	2	3	4	5
HUrried TUBS ONE	aCROSS CONcrete WASn't	TURNed	Alleyway	STARted DARK ARCHway PLANT
6	7	8	9	
WALK	DRIZZling INto SIt WINter	WENT BENches WET	STREET PREcincts SEEN	

1.11

ANSWERS

This task anticipates some segments that are dealt with in Tasks 1.12–1.14.

1 PASSED /ɑː/ FAshionable /æ/
  SHOPS /ɒ/ DREsses /e/
  BRIGHT PLAStic /æ/
  LIGHTS FIgures /ɪ/
  BARgains /ɑː/ VIdeos /ɪ/

FRIdges	/ɪ/	LEFt	/e/
HUNdreds	/ʌ/	GIFt	/ɪ/
SHOES		HOlly	/ɒ/
GIVE	/ɪ/	SNOWmen	
PRIces			

2
LASt	/ɑː/	THOUGHT	/ɔː/
SHOp	/ɒ/	PUB	/ʌ/
JUST	/ʌ/	FIRST	/ɜː/
DOORS	/ɔː/	LEFT	/e/
COULD		perHAPs	/æ/
TELL	/e/	THERE	
MARket	/ɑː/		

The simple vowels /uː/ in 'SHOES' and /ʊ/ in 'COULD' can be added to the table begun in Task 1.9. The diphthongs in 'BRIGHT', 'LIGHTS', 'PRIces', 'SNOWmen' and 'THERE', are dealt with in the next task.

1.12

Observation of lip movement is suggested as one way of appreciating the shift in the vocal organs that distinguishes a diphthong.

1.13

Ten out of the eleven tone units have one simple vowel and one diphthong in their prominent syllables. The pairs of sounds that are brought together in this way are *not* generally of the kind that are often said to 'cause confusion', e.g. the *bid/bead* contrast. The idea is that students focus upon getting a better 'feel' of the difference between simple vowels and diphthongs.

ANSWERS

1 // EVeryone got OUT //

2 // she WASn't sure WHERE //

3 // it was TOO LATE //

4 // there were STREET LIGHTS //

5 // NO CARs admitted //

6 // she was just CLOsing the DOORS //

7 // she'd NO iDEA //

8 // perHAPs they'd know THERE //

9 // i WENT round to a SIDE door //

10 // it was just HALF past FIVE //

11 // she was emPLOYED there during the HOlidays //

Number 7 has two diphthongs.

1.14

Students should identify diphthongs by noticing whether there is a change in the position of the tongue or lips.

DIPHTHONG TYPE

1	2	3	4	5	6	7
OUT	SNOWmen NO CLOsing	WHERE THERE	LATE	LIGHTS SIDE FIVE	iDEA	emPLOYED

1.15

See Note 8 on self-diagnosis on pages 6–7.

Unit 2 Help!

The aim of the first part of this unit is to begin to make students aware that speakers can choose *different tones* in tone units and that the choice has an effect upon the way the tone unit works in a conversation. Only the **falling** and the **rising** tones are introduced at this stage. If the activity in the 'Listening for meaning' section is carried out in pairs, students will have experience of using much of the language of the original conversation before going on to attend specifically to pronunciation.

Summary

1 The information we parcel up into tone units serves to further a speaker's purpose in either of two ways:
   a) It may refer to some part of the message about which speaker and listener are both already aware; that is to say, it may make clear what the speaker assumes is already common ground between them.
   b) Alternatively, it may include information which is not yet shared. When we say we 'tell' someone something, we usually take that to mean that we have information that the other person doesn't yet have.
2 We show which of these two functions a tone unit has by using a particular **tone** (the technical name we give to the pitch movement that begins at the tonic syllable).
3 Most of the simple consonant sounds that English uses can be found, and practised if necessary, before the vowel of a prominent syllable.
4 Many of the difficulties that people have in making these sounds arise from what particular type they are – **voiced** or **voiceless**, **plosive** or **fricative** – and it often helps to pinpoint problems if this is recognised.
5 The consonants encountered in this unit are:

	Voiced	*Voiceless*
Plosive	/d/ /g/ /b/	/t/ /k/ /p/
Fricative	/ʒ/ /v/ /z/ /ð/	/ʃ/ /f/ /s/ /θ/

Listening for meaning

The activity of relating David's directions to the map will give students the necessary familiarity with the route before beginning detailed work on the conversation.

ANSWERS

	Place	*Directions*
1	Cul de sac	Don't turn here.
2	Underpass	Go under.
3	Traffic lights	Turn right.
4	Crossroads	Get in right-hand lane.
5	T-junction	Turn right.
6	Mini-roundabout	Take the first exit.

Listening to intonation

2.1

Before beginning work on tone, it may be useful to make a link with the work on prominence in Unit 1 by comparing the first piece with the 'market street' example in Task 1.7.

Pieces (2)–(4) enable students to listen contrastively to falling and rising tones. Emphasise that it is at the *last* prominent syllables (i.e. the *only* prominent syllable if there is only one!) in the tone unit where the significant pitch movement occurs, and that it continues to the end of the tone unit.

The only new transcription convention introduced in this unit is an arrow placed at the beginning of the tone unit to show which tone is used. The underlining which was introduced in Unit 1 serves as a reminder of where the pitch movement begins. (The reason for not putting the arrow here is given in Note 17 on pages 11–12.)

2.2

The purpose of this task is to give practice in recognising falling and rising tones and in using the newly introduced transcription conventions. If the task is carried out conversationally, students are likely to repeat some of the tone units as part of their decision-making procedure, and this is obviously to be encouraged. If some students anticipate the next unit by using a fall-rise where the recording has a rise, this can be accepted without comment at this stage.

ANSWERS

1 // ↘ you must TURN <u>RIGHT</u> // ↘ and you'll see a MIni

ROUNdabout // ↘ and you want the FIRST <u>EX</u>it //

2 // ↘ you must TURN <u>RIGHT</u> // ↗ THEN you keep <u>GO</u>ing //

↗ unTIL you <u>COME</u> // ↘ to a MIni <u>ROUN</u>dabout // ↗ and ON the

<u>ROUN</u>dabout // ↘ you want the FIRST <u>EX</u>it //

Comparison of (1) and (2) should set students thinking about possible reasons for using rising rather than falling tones in these particular examples. It will be enough if they notice that version (1), that is to say, the version without the rising tone additions, tells an enquirer exactly the same as the longer version with them. The content of the tone units with rising tone tells nothing that the enquirer doesn't already know.

2.3

If this version is compared with the recorded version that begins the unit, it will be found that it is not an exact copy; in particular, some of the hesitations and false starts have been removed to make the repeated use of rising tones more obvious.

Time should be spent on the pairwork, each contribution from Mandy and David being worked on separately if necessary. Some pairs could then be asked to read the complete conversation for the whole class to hear.

By now, there may be more ideas about the significance of rising tone. Probably the most useful suggestion would be to the effect that at this stage in the conversation neither of the speakers is telling anything that the other doesn't know already.

2.4

This replay of material from Unit 1 is intended to provide a contrast. It shows the very different effect that the repeated use of falling tone has.

2.5

ANSWERS

1 // ↗ come OUt of the <u>CAR</u> park // ↘ and TURN <u>RIGHT</u> //

2 // ↗ AFter a little <u>WHILE</u> // ↘ you'll see a TURning on your <u>LEFT</u> //

3 // ↘ I'M <u>SO</u>rry // ↘ it's the <u>SE</u>cond turning // ↘ it's <u>NOT</u> // ↗ the <u>FIRST</u> // ↘ so that's the <u>SE</u>cond turning // ↗ on your <u>LEFT</u> //

4 // ↗ and if you GO round <u>THERE</u> // ↘ you'll see some <u>PLAY</u>ing fields // ↘ on your <u>RIGHT</u> //

In (1) the instruction given is to 'turn right', and this has a falling tone. If you were in a car park and hoping to get anywhere you would hardly need telling that you must 'come out of the car park'. The rising tone in (1) indicates that this much can be taken for granted. The instruction that cannot be taken for granted is to 'turn right', and this has a falling tone. 'After a little while' is similarly uninforming in (2); here it is the new instruction to look for 'a turning on your left' that has a falling tone. By the time we reach (3), 'the first turning on your left' has been mentioned. Neither of the two tone units that contain 'first' and 'left' adds anything new: they therefore have rising tones. The tone units in which the speaker corrects himself, however, have falling tones: 'I'm sorry . . . it's the second turning' (twice). In (4), most listeners would have already assumed that they must 'go round there'. The speaker would hardly have taken so much trouble over exactly which turning he meant if he was *not* going to tell them to do so. The rest gives new guidance as to what to look out for and on which side of the road it will be. In general, *what needs to be told* has *falling* tones; *what can be assumed to be already understood* has *rising* tones.

In this task, there are some examples of tone units which run together without anything that we can identify as a break:

// ↘ it's <u>NOT</u> [//] ↗ the <u>FIRST</u> //

// ↘ so that's the <u>SE</u>cond turning [//] ↗ on your <u>LEFT</u> //

The reason for counting each of these as two tone units rather than one is that there are two tonic syllables and hence two different choices of tone. 'First' and 'left' are treated as common ground. What needs to be told is that it is *not* the first turning but the *second*.

2.6

This exercise in prediction should be done as a cooperative task if possible.

ANSWER

// ↗ the <u>THING</u> to look <u>OUT</u> for // ↘ is the <u>PLAY</u>ing fields // ↗ and

SOON after you've <u>PASSED</u> them // ↘ you'll GO under an

<u>UN</u>derpass // ↗ <u>AF</u>ter <u>THAT</u> // ↗ HANG <u>ON</u> // ↘ you'll BE in

hospital <u>LANE</u> // ↘ you'll <u>KNOW</u> // ↗ it's hospital <u>LANE</u> //

↘ because of the <u>HOS</u>pital // ↘ it's a BIG vic<u>TO</u>rian building //

↘ on your <u>LEFT</u> // ↗ and at the <u>EN</u>d of <u>THERE</u> // ↘ you'll COME

to some <u>TRA</u>ffic lights //

Note: This is the version on the cassette, but some variations could easily be justified. For instance, if Hospital Lane happened to have been mentioned earlier in the conversation we could have:

// ↘ and after <u>THAT</u> // ↗ you'll be in <u>HOS</u>pital <u>LANE</u> //.

The request to 'Hang on' is introduced as something the listener would expect to do without being told: a possible substitution of falling tone would make it sound like a warning that the instructions are not yet complete or that the speaker is about to go back and change the instructions.

The final stage of the task can be done in pairs, with students comparing the versions they have worked out separately.

2.7

In carrying out this task, students should recognise that some parts of each answer:

1 repeat something that was said in the question (perhaps in other words);
2 are therefore spoken with a rising tone.

The examples provide useful practice in producing a rising tone.

ANSWERS

1 // ↗ i THINK the place you're <u>LOO</u>king for // ↘ is in COllege <u>LANE</u> // ↘ it's a RIGHT <u>TURN</u> // ↘ by the <u>SHELL</u> station //

2 // ↗ you'll FIND <u>THAT</u> // ↘ on the SAME side of the <u>ROAD</u> //

3 // ↘ i'm aFRAID <u>NOT</u> // ↗ if you GO down <u>THERE</u> // ↘ you WON'T get <u>A</u>nywhere // ↘ it's a <u>CUL</u> de sac //

4 '// ↗ well the PROBlem <u>IS</u> // ↘ there are <u>ROAD</u>works // ↘ there's a LOt of con<u>GES</u>tion // ↗ in the <u>CEN</u>tre //

5 // ↘ <u>NO</u> // ↗ i THINK the map you've <u>GOT</u> // ↘ MUST be an <u>OLD</u> one // ↗ COllege <u>LANE</u> // ↘ is in the NEW de<u>VE</u>lopment area //

6 // ↘ aBOUt a <u>MILE</u> // ↗ it's NOT very <u>FAR</u> // ↘ it's the <u>TRA</u>ffic // ↗ that's the BIggest <u>PROB</u>lem // ↗ at THIS time of <u>DAY</u> //

Here, too, alternative treatments are possible. For instance, in (4), if both speakers knew about the present traffic problems in the area, we might have:

// ↗ there's a LOT of con<u>GES</u>tion // ↘ in the <u>CEN</u>tre //

meaning something like 'It's just as bad there as it is here!'

Any kind of prediction depends upon our first making assumptions about the background to the conversation. If the students have sufficient confidence at this stage, it will be instructive to discuss the implications of any alternatives that they produce.

2.8

Some learners have difficulty in placing tonic syllables early in the tone unit. This task is a largely mechanical exercise in doing just that, with both falling and rising tones.

2.9

The use of cassette-recorders for this role play will probably add to its value. It will give them a chance to listen carefully to their own choice of tones and to discuss the effects of the choices in a more open situation than those provided by most tasks in the course. Since they have considerable freedom in putting together their responses, they will not be able to make point-by-point comparisons with the recorded version. They should be clear that reasons for choosing one tone or the other arise from the way their own conversation develops. The measure of correspondence with the recorded conversation is of little importance.

The transcript of the recorded version is as follows:

// ↘ well you'll HAVE to go <u>BACK</u> // ↗ GO down college <u>LANE</u> //

↘↗ PASt the <u>TECH</u>nical college // ↘ BACK to the <u>CROSS</u>roads //

↘ GO straight <u>O</u>ver // ↗ <u>THERE</u> // ↗ Over the <u>CROSS</u>roads //

↘ WHERE you've <u>COME</u> from // ↘ THEN turn <u>LEFT</u> // ↘ into

WIllow <u>ROAD</u> // ↘ that's con<u>TIN</u>uing // ↘ along the ROAD you were

on be<u>FORE</u> // → and <u>GO</u> on // ↗ DOWN <u>THERE</u> // ↗ unTIL you

<u>COME</u> // ↘ to a BIG <u>ROUN</u>dabout // ↘ take the <u>SE</u>cond // ↗ <u>EX</u>it //

↘ and you'll be in a LONG straight <u>ROAD</u> // ↗ go RIGHT to the

<u>END</u> // ↘ and THEN turn <u>LEFT</u> //↗ and THAT will <u>TAKE</u> you //

↗ to the MIni <u>ROUN</u>dabout // ↘ you're <u>LOO</u>king for // ↘ ON park

<u>ROAD</u> //

Listening to sounds

2.10

All the tasks in this part of the unit should be directed first of all towards getting the target consonant right. On a second run through, however, it may be possible to focus upon both the target consonants and the vowels which were targeted in Unit 1.

ANSWERS

CONSONANTS AT THE BEGINNING OF PROMINENT SYLLABLES

1	2	3	4	5	6
GO GOing GOT	TOLD TURning TECHnical TERminus TUBS TELL	DOWN DONE DARK DOORS	FIRST beFORE PHONE	CUL de sac CONcrete	PASt PARK PASSED PUB
7	8	9	10	11	12
SEcondary SERvice SIT SAW SAID SOrry herSELF	THAT THAT'S THERE	BY BENches	SHOPS SHOE SHE	VIdeos VIsitor	THINGS THOUGHT

2.11 and 2.12

These tasks are concerned with the voiced/voiceless distinction between consonants. The main purpose is to provide help with the self-diagnosis of problems; if a student's native language does not have this particular distinction, one sound – or several sounds in one of the groups – may need to be worked upon.

2.12 ANSWERS

Voiced	Voiceless
/d/	/t/
/g/	/k/
/b/	/p/
/ʒ/	/ʃ/
/v/	/f/
/z/	/s/
/ð/	/θ/

2.13 and 2.14

The focus here is upon the plosive/fricative distinction. The intention is, once more, to make it easier for students to pinpoint sounds, or groups of sounds, on which they need to concentrate.

2.14 ANSWERS

Plosives	Fricatives
/p/ /k/ /d/ /t/ /g/ /b/	/s/ /ð/ /f/ /ʃ/ /v/ /θ/

Unit 3 What's new?

This unit introduces the fall-rise tone as an alternative way of referring to a part of the message that is presumed to be already part of the shared background of speaker and hearer. In the recorded conversation and also in the suggested 'Listening for meaning' activity, the emphasis is upon talking about what can be jointly remembered. This is a context in which the fall-rise naturally occurs very often. Students might be asked to suggest other situations in which this kind of conversational reconstruction of the past can be heard. For instance, two people might be trying to recall the detailed plot of a film that both have seen in the past, but which neither remembers completely.

Summary

1 We often use a **fall-rise** tone when the tone unit refers to information that we think is already shared by our listener.
2 Both the fall-rise and the rising tones enable us to make clear that we are making this kind of reference instead of proclaiming some part of the message as *not* shared.
3 There is a difference in the effect we produce by using one or the other of the **referring tones**, but we are concerned in this unit only with their similarity.
4 The length of so-called 'long' vowels and of diphthongs varies quite considerably. They fit their description most reliably when they occur in a prominent syllable at the end of a tone unit.
5 In this position some speakers find it easier if they produce a further sound after a vowel or diphthong from what we call in this course the **NLA** (Nasals, Laterals and Approximants) group.

Listening for meaning

The task of 'cooperative recall' that is suggested here will provide a warming-up experience of the kind of activity that the unit concentrates upon, without yet making any explicit reference to intonation.

ANSWERS

Arthur	A senior member of staff, who is rather secretive and set in his ways.
Jane	Formerly worked 'upstairs'. She left about two years ago and no one from the office has been in contact with her since.
Ted	Worked with Jane upstairs, and has so far failed to get a different job.
Mary	She is Irish and works in the Accounts Department. She started to work in the office after Tony left, so he doesn't know her.
Sarah	She also works in Accounts.
Jane Harrison	Tony seems to be implying that she worked in Accounts, too, but it is not very clear.
Angela	She was 'rather serious'.
John Fellows	He was moved to Head Office at about the same time as Tony left. It is said that he is doing very well.

Listening to intonation

3.1

1 // ↘ you reMEMber that FRIENd of his though // ↘ the GUY who came from LIverpool // ↘ he ALways came on FRIdays // ↘ and NObody quite knew WHY //

2 // ↘ he had a nasty ACcident of some sort // ↘ in his CAR //

These two extracts are brought together to show how tones distinguish the 'shared understanding' part of the message (said with fall-rises) from the 'unshared' part (said with falling tones).

Nothing needs to be added to what was said about this distinction in Unit 2. The main purpose of the tasks in this unit is to get students used to recognising and producing a fall-rise tone as an alternative way of 'referring'. The reason for there being alternatives is dealt with in Units 5 and 6.

3.2

Each example here refers to something that the speaker assumes the listener knows about. Students should be told to cover up the explanatory paragraph that follows the examples until they have first found their own reasons for the fall-rise tone.

In most cases the tone unit continues after the tonic syllable. When students repeat, they should ensure that the 'fall-rise' is distributed over the whole of what remains. There may be a tendency to treat the fall and the rise parts of the tone as two separate pitch movements and consequently to introduce an unwanted tonic syllable: the fall-rise tone becomes two tone units with a fall followed by a rise. Provision is made for practising the kind of extended pitch movement they need in Task 3.8.

3.3

This, and Task 3.4 are exercises in prediction.

ANSWERS

1 // ↘↗ you KNOW everything's <u>CHANGED</u> now // ↘↗ the SEcond <u>FLOOR'S</u> // ↘ comPLETEly <u>DIFF</u>erent //

2 // ↘↗ those THREE little offices that <u>WERE</u> there // ↘ they've <u>GONE</u> //

3 // ↘↗ you KNOW that horrible <u>CO</u>rridor we had // ↘↗ and the little <u>ROOM</u> // ↘↗ where the <u>STOVE</u> was // ↘ <u>THAT</u>'s all <u>GONE</u> // ↘ it's all PLUSH carpet and <u>EA</u>sy chairs down there // ↗ <u>NOW</u> //

3.4

ANSWERS

// ↗ WAIT a <u>MI</u>nute // ↘↗ there was the <u>POST</u> room // ↘↗ and then there was <u>AR</u>thur's place // ↘↗ and there was the <u>PHO</u>tocopying room // ↘ <u>WHERE</u>'s <u>AR</u>thur // ↘ <u>NOW</u> //

The kind of 'thinking aloud' activity that this example demonstrates shows another conversational use to which the 'not news' meaning of the referring tone can be put. The tendency to substitute a rising tone may be greater in this example because students may have been taught that this is the proper intonation to use with a 'list'. The intonation of lists is like the intonation of questions: it works in the same way and is subject to the same kind of variation as is intonation in any other situation.

3.5

In each of these examples, Speaker B begins by replying to something he or she has inferred from Speaker A. For instance, in reply to 'Can I help you?' in (1), Speaker B says:

// ↘ WHAt i'm ACtually looking for //

which amounts to saying 'I assume you are intending to ask me what I am looking for. Well, I am looking for (Market Street)'. This way of prefacing a reply makes it possible to introduce a reservation. In (3) 'If I remember correctly . . . ' says, in effect, 'I assume you will be satisfied if I tell you where I *think* she said she was going to live.' The speaker's uncertain memory is treated as though it were something that the person who asked the question had already taken into account.

ANSWERS

1 // ↘ WELL // ↘ WHAt i'm ACtually looking for // ↘ is MARket street //

2 // ↘ WELL // ↘ WHAt i suGGEST // ↘ is that you USE the RINGroad //

3 // ↘ if I remember coRRECtly // ↘ she's LIving somewhere in KENT //

4 // ↘ OH // ↘ ALL the SEnior staff // ↘ are on the GROUND floor //

5 // ↘ I think FRIday's // ↘ the BEST time // ↘ IF you want to catch tom IN //

3.6 and 3.7

These two tasks provide practice in making an appropriate choice of proclaiming tone or referring tone, the first in interaction with recorded material and the second in interaction with a partner. At least one of these should be worked upon long enough to achieve a reasonable resemblance to the recorded version.

3.8

This task is provided principally to give practice in physically producing fall-rise tones. Some students may not need to spend much time on it. Those who do, should be encouraged to think about its meaning in the context provided by this unit, and upon the 'feel' of producing it, rather than just listening to what it sounds like.

3.9

This exercise in collaborative recall can be expected to encourage the use of fall-rise tones in an unscripted conversation. The aim is to get students to realise that they are using fall-rises when they perform this kind of task.

Listening to sounds

3.10 and 3.11

It is better to focus upon the length of vowels when they occur in this target position (at the end of a prominent syllable which is also at the end of a tone unit). Note that in this respect, diphthongs count as 'long' sounds.

3.12 and 3.13

The use of those sounds that are grouped together as 'NLA' consonants is introduced. The reason for doing it here is that one of the major differences of some non-RP varieties of English results from the production of one or other of these consonants after a vowel in Target Position 3.

3.14

This task, which compares tone-unit-final long vowels with diphthongs, is intended to help students get the characteristic 'feel' of the two kinds of sound. As with nearly everything else in the Part 2s of units, some students will need this more than others.

ANSWERS

Diphthongs			*Long vowels*		
1	... KNOW	/nəʊ/	2	... KEY	/kiː/
4	... TRY	/traɪ/	3	... MORE	/mɔː/
5	... BOY	/bɔɪ/	7	... FAR	/fɑː/
6	... aWAY	/əweɪ/	8	... NEW	/njuː/
9	... THERE	/ðeə/			

3.15

The purpose of introducing alternatives here is certainly not to make things more difficult for students! It is rather to reassure them that whichever pronunciation they find easier is equally acceptable.

Unit 4 Finding out or making sure?

In this unit referring and proclaiming tones are used in situations where speakers need to 'ask' something. (Earlier units have been concerned only with 'telling'.)

Summary

1 Whether you are **telling something** or **asking, referring tones** and **proclaiming tones** retain their essential meanings.
2 When you are telling something, a referring tone means that this part of the message is already shared. Saying it will not, therefore, impart any new information. When you are asking, it means that you assume this part of the message is shared but you want to make sure by asking your listener to confirm it.
3 When you are telling something, a proclaiming tone means that you do not think your listener has certain information that you possess. When you are asking, it means that your listener has some information that you do not possess: you need to find out.
4 When you ask questions for mainly social reasons, you usually use referring tones.
5 Replies, or parts of replies, which do not answer questions directly, have referring tones.
6 There is no clearly perceived release when a plosive consonant is the first element in a final cluster of consonants.
7 If the first element of a final cluster of consonants is voiced, the second is voiced also. There is similar correspondence between voiceless elements.

Listening for meaning

CONVERSATION 1 ANSWERS

Information that the customer might be expected to have includes the title, author, publisher and date of publication.

Listening to intonation

4.1

All these examples have fall-rise versions of a referring tone. Before going on to the explanation that follows this task, students could be given a chance to try to work out for themselves why referring tone is very often used with enquiries like these. They may notice (or be led to notice) that in each case the speaker is, in effect, *checking a reasonable assumption*: customers *usually* refer to books by title, one would *normally* look in the biography section for that kind of book, and so on . . .

4.2

This task is intended to give practice in using the fall-rise tone in some more enquiries where a speaker might be said to be more likely to be 'making sure' than 'finding out'.

They are also the kinds of enquiry in which the fall-rise is more likely to occur than the rise: where the enquirer is less likely to adopt a dominant stance. (The differing effect of using the two is shown later in Unit 6. The central point of this unit is made more clearly if this complication is avoided by using only the fall-rise version.)

CONVERSATION 2 ANSWERS

The 11.48 train to York has been cancelled.
The next direct train is at 13.20 and gets to York at 15.10.
An alternative train, which involves changing at Manchester, leaves from platform two in five minutes' time. It gets to York at 14.48.
A ticket bought for the direct route is valid for this route as well.

4.3

All these examples have falling tones. The fact that in each of these cases the speaker is likely to have no previous expectations will probably not be difficult to establish. Note, though, that in order to do this, it is necessary to refer to the specific encounter between traveller and enquiry clerk that we have in mind. It is only by trying to fill in the here-and-now background of the conversation that we are able to say whether speakers need to find out something new or merely to check on what they believe to be the case.

Two points may need stressing here:

1 There is no way in which we can recognise a 'finding out' or a 'making sure' enquiry, simply by looking at it in its written form. It always depends on whether the speakers have – or, in many cases, *act as though they have* – previous expectations. (Task 4.6 is concerned with some occasions when we regularly *act as though* we have previous expectations for social reasons.)

2 It seems to be a fact that *yes/no* questions are more often used as 'making sure' enquiries, while *wh-* questions are more often used to 'find out'. While there is no harm in noting these tendencies, any suggestion that it is the 'question type' that decides the intonation should be avoided. Counter-examples can be found in the examples used in this unit. Moreover, as we said earlier, 'asking' of either kind is frequently accomplished with items that do not look like 'questions' at all.

4.4

This task provides practice in saying 'finding out' enquiries, using examples that might very well fit into 'finding out' situations. It is possible, however, that alert students will recognise that some of them could equally well have a referring tone and so work as 'making sure' enquiries: that is to say, they may anticipate the explanation that follows the task.

4.5

After trying out the pairs of examples and getting the feel of the difference between the two kinds of enquiry, students can usefully be encouraged to imagine circumstances in which these enquiries might take one or other of the possible forms. For instance (4) is most likely to be spoken with referring tone because there is a general expectation that it will be the person you are phoning who will answer; 'making sure' is then little more than a way of opening the conversation. But if it doesn't sound like David's voice, the caller might well feel that it is necessary to 'find out' whether she has got the right person before going on.

Some discussion of **phatic communion** – the use of language to establish a comfortable social relationship, or to accord with the standard ritualistic demands of the culture – might be useful here. It is generally true that, because the purpose of our phatic routines is to emphasise the 'togetherness' of the participants, the referring tone is the natural choice.

4.6

The first two examples will provide an opportunity for discussing the difference between 'real' enquiries and 'social' ones. The doctor may need to 'find out' in order to know whether to continue the same treatment. If, however, the friend had used a similar proclaiming tone, the implication might have been something like 'Your state of health is a matter of concern to me. I don't know whether you are fit enough to . . . ' While this could sometimes be interpreted as sympathetic concern, there are circumstances in which it would be a discouraging thing to say. Using a 'making sure' enquiry treats the other person's state of health as something far less likely to be a problem: it is therefore the natural choice when it is not intended as a 'real' enquiry.

4.7

While 'making sure' enquiries often sound more friendly than 'finding out' enquiries, there are some occasions when it is better not to suggest that you have made an assumption about the answer already. Enquiries beginning with 'perhaps' or 'I wonder' avoid doing this.

ANSWERS

3 // ↘ well i'm RAther <u>BU</u>sy // ↘↗ just at <u>PRE</u>sent // ↘ per<u>HAP</u>s you wouldn't mind <u>WAI</u>ting for a few minutes //

4 // ↘↗ aCCORding to the <u>IN</u>dicator board // ↘↗ the NEXT train to <u>YORK</u> // ↘ has been <u>CAN</u>celled // ↘ but NO one seems to know <u>WHY</u> // ↘ i WONder whether <u>YOU</u> can tell me //

4.8

In this task the focus is upon the reply rather than the enquiry. The essential point is that when you provide the information you are asked for you generally use a proclaiming tone; but if you respond without giving that information you use a referring tone. This is often a conversational device for stopping short of giving the information you think the asker wants. There may be various reasons for side-stepping the issue: you may simply not know the answer, or you may have your own reasons for not wanting to give it. By saying:

// ↘↗ well it <u>COULD</u> be //

the customer really says what the assistant could be expected to know already: if the assistant hadn't thought it *could be* a recent publication she would scarcely have asked!

ANSWERS

3 // ↗ i <u>THINK</u> so // ↗ the PROBlem <u>IS</u> // ↘ i'm NOT quite <u>SURE</u> //

4 // ↗ well it's ONE way at the <u>MO</u>ment // ↘ because they're doing

a LOt of <u>SE</u>wer work //

5 // ↗ NOT <u>REA</u>lly // ↘ <u>NO</u> //

6 // ↗ well he <u>US</u>ed to // ↘ but it's ALL <u>CHANGED</u> // ↗ <u>NOW</u> //

4.9

It is better if students do not look back at Unit 2 but rely upon their memories here. The need to either find out or make sure will then depend genuinely upon whether they think they can remember the location of each place or not.

Listening to sounds

4.10 AND 4.11

Some students have difficulty with consonant sounds that come at the end of a tone unit. This task follows our usual practice of concentrating upon those which are also part of a prominent syllable. The activity of sorting the sounds concerned into the three main types is intended to help students discover whether their problems are restricted to one (or two) of these. Final plosives are, for instance, , difficult for some learners.

The sound /ŋ/ may require some attention.

4.11 ANSWERS

	Voiced sounds	*Voiceless sounds*
NLA sounds	reTURN /n/ aLONG /ŋ/ BELL /l/ GROOM /m/	
Plosive sounds	PUB /b/ ODD /d/ BAG /g/	OUT /t/ BACK /k/ STOP /p/
Fricative sounds	SHOES /z/ FIVE /v/ WITH /ð/	aCROSS /s/ RUSH /ʃ/ BREATH /θ/ LIFE /f/

4.12

Two-consonant clusters in final position in a tone unit are introduced here. Again, the emphasis is upon which particular clusters are difficult for the particular learner.

4.13

A distinction is made here between clusters which begin with an unreleased plosive and those which begin with a continuant. The former type may require special attention from some learners.

ANSWERS

1 *First sound is a continuant*	LEFT /ft/ ASK /sk/ aROUND /nd/ FIND /nd/ THINK /ŋk/ mySELF /lf/ END /nd/ MIND /nd/ SHELF /lf/ FRIEND /nd/
2 *First sound is a plosive*	STOPPED /pt/ ASKED /kt/ SHOPS /ps/ TUBS /bz/ YARDS /dz/

4.14

The so-called 'affricatives', /tʃ/ and /dʒ/, are introduced here as being very similar to the second type recognised in Task 4.13 (/pt/, /kt/ etc.).

4.15–4.18

In these tasks, the common grammatical endings '-ed' and '-s' are used to show how the first element of a cluster affects the second with respect to voicing. By describing the circumstances in which these endings do *not* result in a cluster, one can correct the tendency of some speakers to make them syllabic when they shouldn't be (e.g. 'The bus /stɒped/').

4.16 ANSWERS

1	/t/ (voiceless)	5	/s/ (voiceless)
2	/z/ (voiced)	6	/t/ (voiceless)
3	/t/ (voiceless)	7	/z/ (voiced)
4	/t/ (voiceless)	8	/d/ (voiced)

4.18 ANSWERS

1	/vd/	5	/tʃt/
2	/tɪd/	6	/tɪd/
3	/dz/	7	/tɪd/
4	/sɪz/	8	/pt/

Unit 5 Who is in charge?

This unit is intended to alert students to two separate pronunciation features, both of which are much in evidence in the chairperson's speech. These are:

1 features which result simply from the fact that he is having to assemble the language as he goes along;
2 features that arise from the fact that he is dominant speaker.

Those of the first kind, which are 'accidental', can sometimes get in the way of our hearing the second kind. The early tasks are therefore designed to help students disregard the unavoidable 'untidiness' of much unprepared speech and perceive the significant patterns that are nevertheless present – patterns that are still there when the utterance has been tidied up.

Summary

1 Fluent native speakers, like learners, often have difficulty in putting together the language they need to express their intentions, and this results in the use of **level tones**.
2 The rising version of referring tone is used by **dominant speakers**.
3 Dominant speakers may:
   a) be appointed in advance, as in the case of the chairperson;
   b) hold the position by unspoken agreement for the time being, as in the case of a storyteller;
   c) seek to take control briefly in the course of a conversation in which speaker and listener have equal rights, as in the conversation between Mandy and David in Unit 2.
4 Dominant speakers have a choice: they can either make use of the rising tone to underline their present status as controller of the discourse, or they can refrain from doing so and use the non-dominant fall-rise instead.
5 There are occasions when the choice is not very significant and you can use either tone. There are some circumstances, however, when it is better to assume the dominant role and some when it is better not to. These will receive attention in the next unit.

6 Some vowels are **protected**: they remain more or less constant wherever they occur. Others are **unprotected**: the sound a speaker actually makes can vary considerably from one occasion to another. The most common pronunciation of unprotected vowels is something like /ə/ or /ɪ/, but the reduction to these sounds comes about as a result of speakers not being very concerned about what sound they make: /ə/ and /ɪ/ are not, therefore, to be thought of as targets in the sense that other vowels are.

7 All words of more than one syllable have at least one protected vowel.

8 Monosyllables which are **content words** have protected vowels; those which are **function words** have unprotected vowels.

Listening for meaning

Both the chairperson's style of speech and the special procedures of the occasion may obscure the meaning for some students. The activity of sorting out the essential information conveyed in the speech will allow any problems of understanding to be dealt with before proceeding to pronunciation matters.

ANSWERS

The next meeting will be the Annual General Meeting (AGM).
It will be necessary to elect a new secretary to replace Jane Parks, who is moving to Glasgow.
There will also be elections for some new committee members.
The society is getting into debt, so it will be necessary to increase subscriptions.
This evening's speaker is Dr Agnes Thomson.
She is a graduate of the university where the meeting is taking place.
She has an MA and a PhD from Harvard and has lectured at Hyderabad.
Her speciality is the work of Wittgenstein.
Tonight she is speaking on Wittgenstein and Feminism.

Listening to intonation

It may be necessary to discuss the role of chairperson, and also some of the conventions and vocabulary of this kind of event, before proceeding with this unit. Students will need to see that the chairperson's speech is not ordinary relaxed conversation. They may need help to recognise the uncolloquial nature of much of it: to see, for instance, that the speaker is using set phrases like 'good evening one and all' and 'a good and spirited attendance' rather self-consciously and with mildly humorous intent. If something of the sense that the speech is a bit mannered and contrived is appreciated it will reinforce the point made in Task 5.1.

The part of the speech that is repeated on the cassette sounds like this:

// → ER // ↗ good Evening // → ER // ↗ good EVening to one and ALL // → WELcome // → TO // → OUR // ↗ FEBruary MEEting // → ERM // → and WELcome // → of COURSE to our // ↗ to our REGular // → MEMbers // → and aTTENders // → and SEVeral FAces er // → i can SEE out there // → NOT // ↗ TOO familiar to ME //

5.1

The hesitations and the use of level tones are here associated with the speaker's preoccupation with his choice of words and with the organisation of his language in general: he is feeling his way forward and, from time to time, needs a moment to prepare what he is going to say next.

ANSWERS

2a // ↘ beFORE // ↗ i introduce tonight's SPEAker // → there's ER // ↘ ONE // ↗ important reMINder //

3a // ↘ NEXT month's // ↗ MEEting // → will BE // → OUR // ↘ ANNual GENeral meeting //

4a // → AND er // ↗ on that oCCAsion // → we're HOping for // → a GOOD // → and SPIrited // ↗ aTTENdance //

It is worth stressing the similarity between the planning problems of a native speaker who is using a kind of English that differs from his or her 'normal speech' and those of the non-native speaker. Obviously, neither hesitation nor level tone needs to be taught! It should, however, be reassuring to the learner to understand that his or her own speech will almost certainly exhibit these features at least as frequently as does that of the native speaker, and for very similar reasons. It is not helpful to set oneself impossibly high standards of 'fluency'.

5.2

The frequent use of rising tones remains a conspicuous feature of these extracts after they have been 'tidied up'. This needs to be explained. Firstly, virtually everything the chairperson says and does is part of the taken-for-granted routine of such meetings, so very little of it is proclaimed: one or other of the referring tones is appropriate. The next question is 'Which one?'

The chairperson takes part in the event as someone who has 'control of the conversation' in a rather obvious way. This provides us with a situation within which the special meaning of the rising tone can be appreciated. Students can be asked to suggest other events in which the understood rules of the game make one speaker dominant (e.g. the classroom lesson, the formal interview, etc.). It may be necessary to point out that 'dominance' here has none of the undesirable connotations of 'bossiness' that sometimes attach to the word.

ANSWERS

1a // ↗ JANE <u>PARKS</u> // → has <u>SERVE</u>d us // ↘ <u>MAR</u>vellously for //
→ i <u>THINK</u> it's about // ↘ <u>THREE</u>
<u>YEARS</u> // ↗ <u>NOW</u> //

2a // → she's <u>LEA</u>ving // → to <u>TA</u>ke up a post // ↗ in <u>GLAS</u>gow //
↗ we wish her <u>WELL</u> //

3a // ↘ un<u>FOR</u>tunately // ↗ to<u>DAY</u> // → our a<u>TTEN</u>dance // → i can
<u>SEE</u> is // ↘ <u>NO</u>t as good // ↗ as <u>U</u>sual //

4a // ↗ <u>JUS</u>t a few <u>WORDS</u> // → a<u>BOUT</u> // ↗ her <u>BACK</u>ground //

5a // ↗ she's <u>RE</u>cently re<u>TURNED</u> // ↗ <u>TO US</u> // → <u>FROM</u> a <u>YEAR</u> //
↘ in <u>IN</u>dia //

5.3

This task is introduced here to show how dominant speakers can avoid using the rising tone when circumstances make this desirable. It is probably better not to go into greater detail than that provided in the explanation following the task.   ⟫→

ANSWERS

// ↘↗ ALso // ↘ and THIs is rather // ↗ a SAD note // ↘↗ er the TREAsurer // ↘↗ TELLS me // ↘↗ that we must SERiously consider // → INcreasing // ↘ subSCRIPtions //

To try to explain, tone unit by tone unit, why one or other of the referring tones is used would require an immensely complicated account of the relationships between speaker and listener, and this would certainly not help the learner. The essential point is that, although either will often do equally well, there are some circumstances – to be dealt with later – when one is preferable to the other.

5.4

ANSWERS

1 // ↗ now you KNOW where the Office is // ↗ WHAt i want you to DO // ↗ is to GO to the Office // ↘ and FIND SUsan // ↗ and ASK SUsan // ↘ for the KEY // ↘ to my ROOM // ↗ when you've GOT the KEY // ↗ GO to my ROOM // ↘ and LOOk in the CUPboard // ↗ and IN THERE // ↗ you'll find a ROUND TIN // ↘ with another KEY in it //

2 // ↗ THIS PERson i know // ↘ had JUST been SHOpping // → AND // ↗ she'd JUST FInished // → AND // ↗ she was LOAded up with PARcels // ↗ and STUFF she'd BOUGHT // → AND // ↗ EVeryTHING // → AND // ↗ she was GOing back to her CAR // ↗ IN the CAR park // → and she was GOing aCROSS // ↘ to where she'd LEFt it // ↗ and she SAW SOMEone // ↘ SItting // ↘ in the PAssenger seat // ↘ of her CAR //

3 // ↗ you COME out of the CAR park // ↘ and turn RIGHT // ↗ and AFter you've gone a little WAY // ↘ you'll COME to a ROUNdabout // ↗ go ROUND the ROUNdabout // ↘ and take the

SEcond EXit // ↘ NOT the FIRST // ↘ because THAT will take

you into TOWN // ↗ take the SEcond EXit // ↗ and conTINue

along THERE // ↘ for about a MILE //

Students will probably notice that, although the referring tones are predominantly of the rising kind in these three examples, the alternative fall-rise occurs from time to time. This kind of substitution may happen when they repeat them, though not necessarily in the same places. They should come to see that, provided the dominant stance is generally maintained, the occasional lapse into the more relaxed, non-dominant mode is allowable and sometimes desirable.

Time spent on this task, giving attention to prominence as well as to tone, will provide valuable revision and reinforcement of ground covered in earlier units.

5.5

This task gives further practice in perceiving and producing rising and fall-rise tones in contrasting situations.

ANSWERS

1 // ↗ our SPEAker for this EVening // ↘ is doctor AGnes
   THOMson //
   // ↘ toNIGHT'S SPEAker's // ↘ AGnes THOMson //

2 // ↗ she TOOK her MASter's degree // ↗ and her DOCtorate //
   ↘ at HARvard //
   // ↘ she GOT her MASter's // ↘ and DOCtorate // ↘ in the
   STATES //

3 // ↗ she's WELL KNOWN // ↘ for her WORk on WITTgenstein //
   // ↘ she MADE her NAME // ↘ with some WORk on
   WITTgenstein //

The recorded versions of (4) and (5) are as follows:

4 // ↘ LAdies and GENtlemen // ↗ our SPEAker for this EVening //
   ↘ is doctor AGnes THOMson // ↗ she TOOK her MASter's

degree // ↗ and her <u>DOC</u>torate // ↘ at <u>HAR</u>vard // ↗ and she's

WELL <u>KNOWN</u> // ↘ for her work on <u>WITT</u>genstein //

5A: // ↘↗ the <u>MEE</u>tings // ↘ are PREtty <u>GOOD</u> usually //

  B: // ↘ perHAPS i should come a<u>LONG</u> some time //

  A: // ↘↗ well to<u>NIGHT</u>'s speaker // ↘ is AGnes <u>THOM</u>son //

  B: // ↗ i <u>SEEM</u> to have // ↘ <u>HEAR</u>d of // ↗ <u>HER</u> // ↘↗ is SHE

    <u>BRI</u>tish //

  A: // ↘↗ i <u>THINK</u> so // ↘↗ but she got her <u>MAS</u>ter's // ↘↗ and her

    <u>DOC</u>torate // ↘ in the <u>STATES</u> //

  B: // ↘ WHAT does she <u>TALK</u> about //

  A: // ↘↗ well she <u>MA</u>De her <u>NAME</u> // ↘ with some <u>WORK</u> she did

    on <u>WITT</u>genstein //

5.6

This task reactivates material already worked on in Unit 2 and
requires that students see it from a different point of view. The
possibility of there sometimes being conflicting views as to who is
supposed to be in charge – as, for instance, in the case of a television
interview – could well be raised here. The transcript of the
conversation is as follows:

Mandy: // ↗ now LET me see if i've got it <u>RIGHT</u> // ↗ i need the

           RIGHT hand <u>LANE</u> //

David: // ↗ <u>YES</u> // ↗ RIGHT hand <u>LANE</u> //

Mandy: // ↗ YES //

David: // ↗ BY the SHELL <u>SER</u>vice station //

Mandy: // ↗ <u>YES</u> //

David: // ↗ <u>CO</u>llege <u>LANE</u> //

Mandy: // ↗ <u>YES</u> // ↗ PAST the <u>TECH</u>nical college //

David: // ↗ PAST the <u>TECH</u>nical college // ↗ PAST the <u>PRI</u>mary

           school //

Mandy: // ↗ <u>YES</u> //

5.7

No model is provided for the station announcement. The suggested discussion may well elicit differing views as to whether students like their announcers to be manifestly 'in charge' or not!

Listening to sounds

5.8

This task introduces the distinction between protected and unprotected vowels and stresses the need for not targeting the latter.

5.9

In the examples here all the protected vowels are in prominent syllables, so 'neglect' of the unprotected ones follows naturally from concentration on prominence.

5.10

The examples here have one protected vowel that is not in a prominent syllable. It is necessary here to avoid introducing an unwanted prominence.

ANSWERS

2 m⟨e⟩mbers   3 g⟨e⟩t   4 tr⟨ou⟩ble   5 m⟨i⟩nd   6 h⟨a⟩ve   7 degr⟨ee⟩

5.11

All words with more than one syllable have at least one protected vowel. These can be determined by reference to the citation forms because they coincide there with primary stress. (Words that have two protected vowels are dealt with in Unit 9.)

5.12

Single-syllable content words have a protected syllable. This is often not apparent from the citation forms in dictionaries in which 'stress' is not marked on monosyllables.

➤

ANSWERS

1 // ↗ i went round // ↘ to a side door //

2 // ↘ there's a set of traffic lights there //

3 // ↗ this is a rather // ↘ sad note //

4 // ↘ it's next to the post room //

5 // ↘ it's near to Hurst Street //

6 // ↘ they're here for the first time //

7 // ↘ it's not as good as usual //

8 // ↘ it's a big brick building //

9 // ↘ it's opposite the service station //

10 // ↗ have you looked in the biography section //

11 // ↘ they've installed a coffee machine //

12 // ↗ she's talking about // ↘ her research //

Unit 6 When to take control

The first part of this unit is concerned with some of the circumstances in which it is better to use one tone rather than another. The main focus is upon the two versions of the referring tone, and the choice is related to the question of whether it is better to behave as if you are 'in control' or not. In Task 6.4 the possibility of not using *either* version is introduced: what circumstances would favour the use of a proclaiming tone instead?

Summary

1 When you use referring tones in 'making sure' enquiries, you may be doing so for the benefit of your listener. In that case, it is usually better to use the 'dominant' form, i.e. the rising tone. This includes offers of help which take the form of 'making sure' enquiries.
2 If you are making sure for your own benefit, it is usually better to use the non-dominant form, i.e. the fall-rise tone. This includes occasions when you use 'making sure' to ask for help.
3 When consonant clusters come at the beginning of a prominent syllable, the first sound is usually attached to the preceding syllable. This cannot happen, obviously, if the prominent syllable begins the tone unit.

Listening for meaning

This conversation is very short. Listening for the answers to the three questions should make students familiar enough with its content.

ANSWERS
___

a) In London.
b) At seven this evening.
c) He will phone her at home.

Listening to intonation

6.1–6.3

These three tasks introduce the general idea that it is often a good thing to adopt a 'controlling' role when your aim is to offer help, but that this may not be such a good idea when you are seeking it. It will be seen that this applies whether one is using question-like utterances or some other kind. Students should be encouraged to examine the two sets of examples and work out the 'Who stands to gain?' distinction for themselves if possible.

6.4 and 6.5

The use of either the fall-rise or the rising tone in Tasks 6.1 and 6.2 depends upon a prior decision to refer rather than to proclaim. Some of the examples could well be heard in other circumstances with a proclaiming (i.e. falling) tone instead. This occurs where there is a clear intention of telling, as in // ↘ DON'T WOrry // or of finding out, as in // ↘ IS he THERE //.

6.5 ANSWERS

1 // ↘↗ IS he THERE //   (a)

2 // ↘ could he POssibly // ↘ make it about SEven //   (b)

3 // ↘ is there Anything I can do //   (b)

4 // ↗ DON'T WOrry //   (a)

5 // ↘ is he THERE //   (b)

6 // ↗ COULD he possibly make it about SEven //   (a)

7 // ↗ is there Anything i can DO //   (a)

8 // ↘ DON'T WOrry //   (b)

6.6 and 6.7

These tasks return to the rise/fall-rise distinction. The pair

// ↗ can i HELp you // (6.6)

// ↘↗ CAN you HELp me // (6.7)

provide a useful pattern with which to compare all the examples.

A possible classroom procedure would be to ask students to speak
examples they select from 6.4 and 6.5 alternately.

6.8

In these examples, there is no easy way of describing the effects of
using one form of the referring tone rather than the other. The task is,
therefore, one in making purely aural discriminations. If it proves too
difficult it is probably better not to insist. Having noted some
situations where the choice noticeably *does* affect the relationship
between speaker and listener, it is possible to reassure students that
there are some situations where it doesn't matter much which of these
tones you use.

ANSWERS

The second version has a rising tone where the first has a fall-rise.

1 // ↘ well <u>NO</u> // ↘ it's HIS day in <u>LON</u>don // ↘↗ to<u>DAY</u> //

  // ↘ well <u>NO</u> // ↘ it's HIS day in <u>LON</u>don // ↗ to<u>DAY</u> //

2 // ↘↗ well he's <u>U</u>sually in // ↘ about <u>SIX</u> //

  // ↗ well he's <u>U</u>sually in // ↘ about <u>SIX</u> //

3 // ↘ PREtty <u>GOOD</u> // ↘↗ <u>REA</u>lly //

  // ↘ PREtty <u>GOOD</u> // ↗ <u>REA</u>lly //

4 // ↘↗ if the <u>BA</u>bysitter doesn't let us down //

  // ↗ if the <u>BA</u>bysitter doesn't let us down //

6.9 and 6.10

These tasks exploit a general tendency to use items like 'usually' with a
non-dominant tone at the beginning, but with a dominant tone at the
end. (It would probably be a good idea not to give too much attention
to why this is so.) The purpose of the tasks is simply to provide
practice in alternating the two tones in circumstances where many
speakers, including learners, seem to find the use of one or other of
them easier and 'more natural'.

6.9 ANSWERS

'Usually' has a fall-rise tone at the beginning of the answer, and a rising tone at the end of the answer.

6.10 ANSWERS

1 // ↘↗ Usually // ↘ it's about <u>SIX</u> //

   // ↘ it's about <u>SIX</u> // ↗ <u>U</u>sually //

2a // ↘↗ <u>AC</u>tually // ↘ it's called HOSpital <u>LANE</u> //

2b // ↘ it's called HOSpital <u>LANE</u> // ↗ <u>AC</u>tually //

3a // ↘↗ e<u>VEN</u>tually // ↘ it led to a peDEStrian <u>PRE</u>cinct //

3b // → it <u>LED</u> // ↘ to a peDEStrian <u>PRE</u>cinct // ↘↗ e<u>VEN</u>tually //

4a // ↘↗ as FAR as i can re<u>MEM</u>ber // ↘ it was a COUPle of <u>YEAR</u>s ago //

4b // ↘ it was a COUPle of <u>YEAR</u>s ago // ↗ as FAR as i can re<u>MEM</u>ber //

5a // ↘↗ at THIS time of <u>DAY</u> // ↘ it will be <u>DREAD</u>ful //

5b // ↘ it will be <u>DREAD</u>ful // ↗ at THIS time of <u>DAY</u> //

6a // ↘↗ if I were <u>YOU</u> // ↗ i should <u>WAIT</u> // ↘ until AFter the <u>RUSH</u> hour //

6b // ↗ I should <u>WAIT</u> // ↘ until AFter the <u>RUSH</u> hour // ↗ if I were <u>YOU</u> //

In (3b) there is a fall-rise, not a rising tone – a reminder that what we are dealing with here is no more than a tendency. There is no question of one of the versions being the 'correct' one.

6.11

ANSWERS

1 // ↘↗ JONson and <u>JON</u>son limited // ↘↗ GOOD <u>MOR</u>ning //
   ↗ CAN i <u>HEL</u>p you //

2 // ↘↗ we <u>DO</u> have a mister robertson // ↗ <u>YES</u> //

3 // ↘ WHO is it CAlling // ↗ PLEASE //

4 // ↘ oh YES // ↗ ONE MOment mister jordan // ↘ i'll SEE if he's
IN //

5 // ↗ good MORning // ↘↗ DO you have a mister RObertson there
please //

6 // ↘↗ COULD i have a WORD with him //

7 // ↘ the NAME'S JORdan // ↘ i'm from JOHN DAvies and co //

Suggested reasons for these choices of tone are:

1 The first two units have fall-rise tones. As a routine acknowledgement
   of the call, followed by a greeting, they do not have the 'dominant'
   tone, but the offer of help does.
2 The agreement that there is someone called Mr Robertson in the
   office has a fall-rise tone, but the telephonist returns to rising tone
   for 'Yes', which is in effect, a further offer of help.
3 'Who is it calling?' is a finding out question and therefore has
   falling tone, but a referring tone is used for the routine (but polite)
   'please'.
4 'Oh yes' with proclaiming tone indicates that the caller has been
   recognised. The last two units, as promises of help, have rising
   tones (Note that 'Mr Jordan' is not a selection in this context, so it
   does not have prominence.)
5 Mr Jordan uses the dominant form of referring tone to return the
   telephonist's greeting but the non-dominant fall-rise to ask about
   Mr Robertson – a request which amounts to asking a favour.
6 The same tone is used to ask to be connected to him and for a
   similar reason.
7 Both these tone units provide information, and therefore have
   proclaiming tones.

6.12

Student B may, for instance, want to find out what the wages will be;
Student A may want to make sure that B is available for weekend
work. Some enquiries could equally well be spoken in either way.

Listening to sounds

6.13–6.17

In accordance with general practice in this course, work on consonant clusters concentrates on cases where these occur as part of a prominent syllable.

In Task 6.13, the focus is upon two-consonant clusters that begin a prominent syllable.

In Task 6.14, students are encouraged to attend to the kinds of sound that go to make up such clusters. By sorting them into two groups, they will have an opportunity of pinpointing some of the difficulties that they, individually, may experience in producing them.

Task 6.15 introduces a situation that presents difficulties for learners: the cluster in question *also* begins the tone unit.

Task 6.16 deals in a similar way with three-consonant clusters, and Task 6.17 presents some cases where spelling conventions can obscure the working of the general principles that are demonstrated in this part of the course.

6.13 ANSWERS

1	PL	10	SW
2	ST	11	CL
3	THR	12	SM
4	ST	13	TR
5	PR	14	TW
6	SP	15	SP
7	PR	16	TR
8	GR	17	SP
9	DR	18	BL

Group 1 /st/ /thr/ /sp/ /sw/ /sm/
Group 2 /pl/ /pr/ /gr/ /dr/ /kl/ /tr/ /tw/ /bl/

6.14 ANSWERS

Group 1:
// i STARted to <u>WALK</u> //
// it's about THREE doors a<u>LONG</u> //
// it SEEMS to be <u>STUCK</u> //
// a SPIrited a<u>TTEN</u>dance //

// you go PAST the <u>SWI</u>mming baths //
// you mean SUsan <u>SMITH</u> //
// our SPEAker for this <u>EV</u>ening //
// the FEminist per<u>SPEC</u>tive //

Group 2:
// WHICH <u>PLAT</u>form is it //
// but there's a <u>PROB</u>lem //
// our PREsent <u>SEC</u>retary //
// she <u>GRAD</u>uated // SOME <u>YEAR</u>s ago //
// she DROVE past the <u>EX</u>it //
// and THAT'S park <u>CLOSE</u> //
// she's <u>TRAV</u>elling // to <u>YORK</u> //
// the THIRteen <u>TWEN</u>ty //
// the TREAsurer of the so<u>CI</u>ety //
// a BLACK <u>CAR</u> //

Unit 7 An urban myth

This unit returns to the question of how we decide where prominent syllables should go. This was raised informally in Unit 1, and it may be helpful to recall some of the discussion that arose from Task 1.8 before proceeding.

Summary

1 Not all words have the same kind of significance in conveying a message. Some carry meanings which can be taken for granted in their contexts, but others occur at points where more than one meaning might reasonably be thought possible. When you make one syllable of a word prominent, you are effectively telling your listener that this word occupies a **selection slot**.
2 A tone unit may have one or two prominent syllables. It may, therefore, have either one or two selection slots.
3 There is no selection unless some significant alternatives are possible: words which are merely alternative labels for what amounts, for present purposes, to the same thing do not count as selective.
4 In considering whether a word occupies a selection slot or not, we always have to consider the total context in which it is being used.
5 The pronunciation of unprotected vowels may vary between a full sound and no sound at all. Most often they tend towards the reduced sounds /ə/ and /ɪ/. It is possible, however, to describe some conditions in which full pronunciation of an unprotected vowel is to be expected:
   a) when it is followed by another vowel;
   b) when it is a diphthong;
   c) sometimes when it occurs in a monosyllable which comes at the end of a tone unit;
   d) when it is selective and therefore made prominent.

Listening for meaning

This part of the unit is rather longer than usual. Discussion breaks – signalled by a bleep on the cassette – are incorporated to make it easier for students to assimilate the narrative.

Listening to intonation

7.1 and 7.2

The thing to establish here is the connection between prominence and the fact that only some of the words in a message represent choices or selections which matter in the present conversation. Reference to note-taking procedures, where predictable words are often missed out, or to 'telegraphese' may help to make the point.

7.2 ANSWERS

1 // ↘ she'd been <u>SHO</u>pping //

2 // ↘ she SAId it was getting <u>LATE</u> //

3 // ↘ she'd GOt out of the <u>LIFT</u> //

4 // → she <u>SAID</u> // ↘ she was feeling <u>GI</u>ddy //

7.3 and 7.4

The same idea is extended here to tone units which have two prominent syllables, and so have two selection slots.

The fact that it is *meaning* selection, not just word selection, that we are interested in is likely to arise in Task 7.4. Many words that do not have prominence can, in fact, be changed for other words and in this sense could be said to represent choices:

// ↘ with a <u>SHO</u>pping bag/basket //

The essential point about alternatives like these is that they do not represent a selection *which has any significance in the present conversation*: they are simply different labels for what amounts, for present purposes, to the same thing.

A useful supplementary exercise would be to try to make word substitutions like these without assigning prominence to them.

7.5

In all these examples, the words without prominent syllables are more or less predictable.

1 // ↘↗ i HOPE you don't <u>MIND</u> // ↘ but i aRRANGed to meet my

<u>DAUGH</u>ter here //

2 // → I said // ↘ WHEN was your daughter supposed to be
COming // ↗ and SHE said // ↘ HALf an HOUR ago //

3 // (and) // ↘ she was WOrried about her DAUGHter //

4 // ↘ it was VEry COLD outside // ↘ it was that VEry cold TIME we
had //

7.6

A strictly logical student might wish to say that the door was either
locked or *not* locked and that (2) is therefore impossible! The answer
to this, of course, is that we do not use the language in accordance
with such strict logic.

7.7

The differences to explain here are:

1b Here 'car park' has been mentioned in the previous tone unit.

2b Here 'hands' has been mentioned in the previous tone unit.

3b 'Drives' has been mentioned previously.

4b 'Back' has been mentioned previously.

7.8

The recorded replies are:

2 // ↗ because she THOUGHT it was called // ↘ hospital ROAD //

3 // ↗ she was SURE he'd be back // ↘ by SEven // ↘ in the
EVening //

4 // ↗ because the diRECT train // ↘ was CANcelled //

5 // ↗ he was TRYing to find a book // ↘ about ARnold //

6 // ↗ they'd turned the OLD coffee room // ↘ into Offices //

The focus here is upon prominence, and students are doing what is
expected of them if they make these words *non-prominent*: 'hospital',
'back', 'train', 'book' and 'coffee'.

Other tone unit divisions and tone choices would achieve this equally well, e.g.:

1 // ↘ because she THOUGHt it was called hospital <u>ROAD</u> //

2 // ↗ she was <u>SURE</u> he'd be back // ↘ by seven in the <u>EV</u>ening //

3 // ↘ because the diRECt train was <u>CAN</u>celled //

4 // ↘ he was TRYing to find a book about <u>AR</u>nold //

5 // ↘ they'd TURNED the old coffee room into <u>O</u>ffices //

It is worth pointing out that each of the five words concerned has a protected vowel. They provide practice, therefore, in preserving the 'full' value of the vowel while avoiding giving it unwanted prominence (see Unit 5).

7·9

This kind of task was included in Unit 1. Students may now be able to associate any difficulties they may have with the fact that intermediate protected vowels (boxed in the transcript below) have to be spoken without prominence. If so, this will lead naturally into Part 2.

1 // ↘ WHEN was your daughter supposed to be <u>CO</u>ming //

2 // ↗ she <u>SAID</u> // ↘ she was going back to her <u>DAUGH</u>ter's //

3 // ↘ she's <u>NE</u>ver // ↘ been late like this be<u>FORE</u> //

4 // ↘ and THEN she took out one of her <u>HANDS</u> //

5 // ↘ OUT from underneath her <u>COAT</u> //

6 // ↗ we'd <u>LIKE</u> to go out // ↘ and search your <u>CAR</u> //

Listening to sounds

7.10

Students may need reminding that a tone unit is usually spoken as a single, pre-planned stretch of speech. This means that any detailed attention that intermediate words may need must be completed, and the whole tone unit mentally prepared for, before it is started. Anything that breaks this continuity will disturb the intended pattern.

7.11–7.15

These tasks are concerned with circumstances in which unprotected vowels regularly retain their full sounds. (See Summary, point 5.)

7.12 ANSWERS

4 why; my   5 my; may   6 where

7.14

The sound that occurs at the end of words like 'many' is here treated as an unprotected vowel whose sound varies between full /iː/ and reduced /ɪ/ and partly depends upon whether it is final in the tone unit.

ANSWERS

In (6b) 'happy' is followed by a vowel so it sounds like /iː/ not /ɪ/.

7.15

Even vowels which are unprotected are given full value when they are used to make a selection.

Unit 8 Can you explain to us . . . ?

The focus of interest in this unit is high key. The recorded interview presents a set of controversial opinions about the place of the motor car in a modern transport system. In this context, assertions are made which are contrary to what might be held to be the popular view. The use of high key is a means of assuming what is expected and simultaneously opposing it; it is therefore easily introduced in this context.

Summary

1 **High key** is marked by a noticeable step up in pitch level at the first prominent syllable in the tone unit.
2 Its function is to mark the contents of the tone unit as being contrary to present expectations.
3 When high key is used to correct or contradict someone, it is good practice to precede it by something said with referring tone.
4 Single-consonant sounds that follow the vowels of a prominent syllable and do not end the tone unit usually sound as if they belong to the next syllable.
5 If there are two or more consonants in this target position the first usually sounds as if it belongs to the prominent syllable and the second as if it belongs to the next syllable.
6 'Middle' consonants in three-consonant clusters in this target position are frequently not sounded.

Listening for meaning

This activity is intended to provoke students to line up on one side or the other in the various arguments that Mr Williams advances. If there is disagreement among members of the class this can be turned to good account in the subsequent discussion of contrast and contradiction.

Listening to intonation

8.1

The effect of high key upon the shape of the fall and the fall-rise tone in a single prominence tone unit is explained, but the corresponding effect upon rising tones is not included. (See Note 19 on recognising key on pages 14–15.)

8.2

The main purpose of this task is to get students used to associating key with a particular prominent syllable.

ANSWERS

1 // i'm SAYing // we SHOULD // res↑TRICT // the MANuFACture // and USE of // ↑ PRIvate motor cars //

2 // for instance their manuFACture // uses UP // other SCARCE // often irre↑PLAceable // NAtural reSOURces //

3 // even if you stray a↑WAY from the town // ↑OUt of town for instance //

8.3

This task is concerned primarily with recognition and imitation, but students can begin to form their own ideas about the significance of high key. One way of approaching the matter is for them to repeat the examples *without* the step up where the arrow is and think about the difference this makes.

8.4

ANSWERS

1 // ↘ we exPECt it to inCREASE mobility // ↘ and it re↑DUces it //

2 // ↘ we're HELd up in TOWN // ↘ and in the ↑COUNtry // ↘ as WELL //

3 // ↘↗ we KNOW the environment is <u>THREA</u>tened // ↘ but we

over↑<u>LOO</u>k it //

4 // ↗ he HASn't always thought like <u>THIS</u> // ↘ he was once a

↑<u>KEEN</u> driver //

The first tone unit, with referring tone, gives a generally shared observation; what is then proclaimed in the second is presented as something as if it were not shared – something which goes against expectations in some way.

8.5

In each of these examples, the first tone unit refers to a belief that is held by some person (or perhaps by people in general), and the second (with high key) contradicts that belief.

ANSWERS

1 // ↘↗ instead of <u>CO</u>pying our mistakes // ↘↗ the <u>LESS</u> de<u>VE</u>loped

countries // ↘ should ↑<u>LEARN</u> from them //

2 // ↘↗ it isn't <u>CLE</u>ver to drive dangerously // ↘ it's irres↑<u>PON</u>sible //

3 // ↘↗ we DON'T need <u>MORE</u> cars on our roads // ↘ we need

↑<u>FEW</u>er //

8.6

In tone units with two prominent syllables, key is indicated at the first of these.

3 // ↘ it's ↑Irres<u>PON</u>sible // ↘ to DRIVE <u>DAN</u>gerously // ↘ it's NOT

<u>CLE</u>ver //

4 // ↘ we ↑CAN't a<u>FFORD</u> // ↘ to waste NAtural re<u>SOUR</u>ces //

↘ we OUGHT to be <u>SA</u>ving them //

Notice that (3) has two prominent syllables in one word:

// . . . Irres<u>PON</u>sible . . . // (see Task 9.16).

8.7 and 8.8

Both tone and key are considered here. The focus is upon avoiding abrupt confrontation when correcting a false belief or assumption.

8.7 ANSWERS

(Slight variations in the wording of the replies are not important, of course, as long as the relevant information features are the same.)

1 // ↘↗ i'm ↑ SOrry // ↘ i ↑DON'T KNOW //

2 // ↘↗ well ↑ ACtually // ↘ at the ↑TRAffic lights //

3 // ↘↗ ↑ DON'T you reMEMber // ↘ i ↑BROUGHT it BACK to you //

4 // ↘↗ unFORtunately // ↘ it stops at ↑EVery STAtion //

5 // ↘↗ well to ↑ TELL you the TRUTH // ↘ i ↑DON'T //

6 // ↘↗ ↑ NOT REally // ↘ she was ↑AFter my TIME // ↘↗ i THINK //

8.8

The fall-rise is used in preference to the rising tone in Task 8.7 because if you are trying to make a contradiction less aggressive you avoid using the 'dominant' rising tone.

8.9

This task uses the students' recollection of the broadcast interview as a context for agreeing and disagreeing.

ANSWERS

2 // ↘ NO // ↘↗ he WASn't the INterviewer // ↘ he was ↑BEing interviewed //

3 // ↘ YES // ↗ THAT'S RIGHT //

4 // ↘↗ not EVeryone // ↘↗ he thought ↑SOME drivers // ↘ were too ↑RECKless //

5 // ↘ eXACtly //

6 // ↘ i ↑DON'T THINK so // ↘ he had been a KEEN driver //
↘ him↑SELF //

7 // ↘ he CERtainly DID // ↘ YES //

8.10

The purpose here is to encourage the same kind of awareness in a more open-ended situation.

Listening to sounds

8.11–8.14

The focus of Part 2 of this unit is upon what happens to consonant sounds after the vowels of prominent syllables. Though students should not be encouraged to think in terms of a break anywhere within the tone unit, awareness of syllable divisions can be helpful. The question posed in the various tasks is whether a consonant should be thought of as belonging to the preceding prominent syllable or to the syllable (usually a non-prominent one) which follows.

8.14 ANSWERS

1 for most of your life
2 just a moment
3 first and foremost
4 it goes via Manchester
5 from platform three
6 we should concentrate on public transport

8.15

Students may need reminding that what is said about Tasks 8.11–8.14 applies to sounds, not spellings. In these examples the composition of the relevant consonant sequence is not apparent from the spelling.

8.16–8.19

All of these tasks are concerned with some kind of 'simplification' which usually occurs around Target Position 4.

⟫→

8.19 ANSWERS

3 sev(e)n o'clock
4 trav(e)lling

5 fashi(o)nable
6 diff(e)rent

Unit 9 Reading aloud

This unit has two distinct aims: to apply what has been learned in earlier units to the special activity of reading aloud; and to introduce low key. In Part 1 students are encouraged to compare two styles of reading. In one, readers treat the text to be read as if it were a report of their own knowledge and present it as a message to listeners, in a way which closely resembles conversation. In the other, the text is treated as no more than a sample of language, whose content and relevance to a listener are not taken into account. In Part 2, the use of low key is practised to convey an *equative* meaning, in contra-distinction to the *contrastive* meaning of high key. (See Note 28 on the meaning of key on pages 21–2.)

Summary

1 When you read aloud, you may assume that: (a) your readers are interested in the message in much the same way as they would be if you were simply speaking to them, or (b) their interest is limited to the words you are using.
   a) In this case, your intonation is similar to what it would be in conversation, except that reading often takes place in situations where readers and listeners have a less detailed understanding of the relevant shared background. It is sometimes necessary, therefore, to be satisfied with a working approximation to an appropriate intonation.
   b) Here, **level tones** are used in a fairly mechanical way, the length of the tone unit depending only upon how many words the reader happens to be able to take in in one 'bite', or how many the listener is expected to deal with.
2 The kind of oblique discourse that results from an engagement with the language rather than with the message is common in language classrooms. It is not only that we tend to 'read out' material using predominantly level tones; teaching and learning language often involve us in talking about such things as 'words' and 'sentences', and when these are the focus of interest, rather than the message, the level tone is often the natural choice.
3 Low key is indicated by a step down in pitch at the first prominent syllable in

the tone unit. It is used to mark the content of the tone unit as 'just what the listener expected'.

4 The citation forms of some words have 'primary' and 'secondary' stresses, that is to say, they follow the pattern of the two-prominence tone unit. When such words occupy a selection slot in a message they have only one prominent syllable. Usually it is the second that is chosen, that is, the one having 'primary' stress in the citation form. If, however, the speech is divided into tone units in such a way that it will be the first prominence in a two-prominence tone unit, then the earlier one (the one having 'secondary' stress) is chosen.

5 Citation forms are sometimes used when we want to foreground a particular *word*, as something we have deliberately chosen. Very often the effect is to impart some kind of emphasis of the kind: 'There is just no other word that will convey what I mean – or feel'.

Listening for meaning

The activity of separating out the news coverage that is given to the actual game from that which is given to other matters should provoke discussion of how news editors decide what is important in such events. Students may well have views about whether the decisions were justified in this particular case.

Listening to intonation

9.1 and 9.2

These tasks encourage students to approach the news item in exactly the same way as they have been approaching other kinds of speech. Prominence and tone choices can be explained on the basis of the kind of understanding the newsreader can expect to have with listeners. The fact that this understanding becomes less reliable as the size of the audience increases can be stressed, however, and the opportunity taken to make the point that no speaker really has access to a listener's mind. All intonation is based upon the best estimate that can be made· about what the two share.

9.1 ANSWERS

a) *today* An evening news item will normally be about a match played 'today', not any other day.

played This is the verb we regularly use when speaking of a match.
match In the expression 'World Cup match' it would be possible to use a different word like 'game', but this would not alter the meaning.
play This is the word that is regularly used in conversations about football to refer to the period of time when the match is actually in progress.
awarded When the referee makes a decision in favour of one team, it is usually said that he 'awards' some advantage to that team.

None of these words occupies a selection slot: usually, there is no likelihood of another word being used; and when an alternative word is possible the change does not bring about a change of meaning.

b) England could only play *against* Spain, so the word does not occupy a selection slot; but the penalty could have been awarded either *against them* or *in their favour*. In the latter case, therefore, it does occupy a selection slot.

c) The newsreader expects listeners to be aware that England had played a World Cup match in Barcelona: all this information is included in tone units that are marked as 'not news' by having a referring tone.

Having been told that their opponents were the cup holders, they do not need to be told that it was 'the champions' they were playing against. After the mention of half time, listeners would usually expect that the next incident to be reported would occur 'soon after play was resumed'. These two pieces of information are therefore spoken with referring tones as well.

9.2 ANSWERS

1 // ⌄ the deCIsion caused UProar // ⌄ among a GROUp of ENGland // ⌄ FANS // ⌄ and THIs in TURN // ⌄ triggered an ANgry // ⌄ resPONSE // ⌄ from some oPPOsing supporters // ⌄ in an adJOIning SECtion // ⌄ of the STAND //

2 // ⌄ the deCIsion caused UProar // ⌄ among a GROUp of england FANS // ⌄ and THIs in TURN // ⌄ triggered an ANgry resPONSE // ⌄ from some oPPOsing suPPORters // ⌄ in an adJOINing SECtion // ⌄ of the STAND //

9.3

This task is intended to show the very different kind of intonation that results from 'reading out' a text on one hand, and 'reading it to' a listener on the other.

ANSWERS

// → suPPORters <u>CLASHED</u> // → DURing <u>PLAY</u> // → in the WORLD cup <u>MATCH</u> // ↘ here to<u>DAY</u> // → <u>ENG</u>land // → had HELD the <u>CHAM</u>pions // → to ONE <u>ONE</u> // ↘ unTIL half <u>TIME</u> // → but <u>SOON</u> // → after PLAY was re<u>SUMED</u> // → a <u>PE</u>nalty // ↘ was a<u>WAR</u>ded a<u>GAINST</u> them // → the de<u>CI</u>sion // → caused <u>UP</u>roar // → among a <u>GROUP</u> // ↘ of england <u>FANS</u> // → and THIs in <u>TURN</u> // → pro<u>VOKED</u> // → an ANgry res<u>PONSE</u> // → from some oPPOsing // → suPPORters // → in an adJOIning <u>SEC</u>tion // ↘ of the <u>STAND</u> //

9.4

This task is intended principally to provide practice in recognition of level tones.

9.5

The significance of level tone, and in particular the way its use arises from the speaker being concerned with language rather than with the message, is worth underlining. Students will appreciate that, since so much of what usually happens in classrooms is concerned with language rather than message, there is likely to have been limited opportunity for practising the kind of intonation one uses in real inter-action with a listener. (See Note 29 on level tone on pages 22–3.)

ANSWERS

1 // ↘↗ SEVeral coMMIttee members // ↘ have <u>AL</u>so expressed // → a <u>WISH</u> to // ↗ STAND <u>DOWN</u> // → <u>FOR</u> // ↘↗ ONE reason or another //

2 // ↘ we <u>ARE</u> // → in <u>FACT</u> // → <u>ER</u> // ↗ GOing into the <u>RED</u> //
→ in a <u>RA</u>ther // ↘ <u>SE</u>rious <u>WAY</u> //

3 // ↗ <u>PO</u>ssibly due to the <u>FLU</u> epidemic // → and <u>ERM</u> // → and and
the <u>STORMS</u> // → and un<u>SEA</u>sonal // ↘ <u>WEA</u>ther out<u>SIDE</u> //

4 // ↘ i think <u>FIRSt</u> and <u>FORE</u>most // → <u>THERE'S</u> // ↘ there's
<u>WHA</u>t i call the environ<u>MEN</u>tal case //

5 // ↘ their manu<u>FAC</u>ture uses up // → <u>O</u>ther // → <u>SCARCE</u> //
↗ often Irre<u>PLA</u>ceable // ↘ <u>NA</u>tural re<u>SOUR</u>ces //

6 // → they're e<u>SSEN</u>tially // ↘ they're e<u>SSEN</u>tially short <u>LIVE</u>d
articles //

All of these seem to include hesitations of the (a) type: the speaker is taking time to put together the language he needs. The use of level tone arises here from two different causes. Mr Williams is presenting complicated opinions in immediate response to questions and is likely to need time to prepare his replies. The journalist is working from a prepared script and is therefore unlikely to do so.

9.6

See Note 8 on pages 21–2 for an account of low key.

Notice that the use of low key indicates an expectation on the part of the speaker. In (1), listeners are expected to know that 'Spain' are 'the present champions'. If they are not expected to know, mid key will be used. Similarly, use of low key for 'the Spanish captain' assumes that this person and 'Marcos' are known to be one and the same. Mid key would assume that it was necessary to tell listeners what Marcos's status was in the team.

9.7

In these examples, too, low key is used in tone units which listeners could be expected to hear as a repetition of information contained in the previous one. Thus:

'in the country' means the same thing as 'out of town'
'the little old lady' means the same thing as 'my passenger', etc.

⏵➔

ANSWERS

1 // ↘↗ TRAffic congestion // ↗ is JUSt as SErious // ↘ OUt of town //
   ↘ in the ↓COUNtry //
2 // ↘ i LOOKed across at my PAssenger // ↘ the ↓LIttle old LAdy //
3 // ↗ JUSt a MOment sir // ↘ i'll ↓SEE if he's IN //
4 // ↘↗ JANE // ↘↗ ↓JANE PARKS // ↘↗ is LEAving // ↘ to go to
   GLASgow //
5 // ↘↗ our NEXT MEEting // ↘↗ the ↓MARCH meeting that is //
   ↘ will be our ANNual GENeral meeting //

It may not be immediately obvious that in (3) the two tone units mean
the same thing, but in the circumstances surrounding a telephone call
like this, 'Just a moment, sir' will usually be taken to indicate that the
telephonist is about to try to make contact with the named person. 'I'll
see if he's in' effectively repeats it.

9.8

This can be regarded as a revision exercise. As a general rule, tasks
require that students pay attention to one feature of pronunciation at
a time. In this task they are asked to attend to a number of such
features.

ANSWERS

1 // ↘↗ our SPEAker for this EVening // ↘↗ doctor ↓AGnes
   THOMson // ↗ is WELL KNOWN // ↘ to MOSt of you //
2 // ↘ YES // ↘ it's the SAME PLATform // ↘ ↓PLATform THREE //
3 // ↘↗ is THAT near the MAPs and things // ↘↗ over ↓THERE //
4 // ↗ ALL the senior STAFF // ↘↗ people like ↓ARthur // ↘ are on
   the GROUND floor //
5 // ↘↗ MARket street // ↘↗ the ↓STREET she was LOOking for //
   ↘ was just a LIttle further aLONG //

9.9

This is an 'open-ended' task intended to give experience in speaking approximately the same material (a) as dictated text, and (b) as a message addressed directly to a listener.

Listening to prominence and sounds

9.10–9.13

These tasks are all concerned with the words which take the form of two-prominence tone units when they are quoted or 'cited' and with what happens to these words when they are used in connected discourse.

Task 9.11 shows the usefulness of such citation forms when one wishes to make clear that one *is* quoting the word: it can be thought of as a way of placing audible 'quotation marks' round it.

Tasks 9.12 and 9.13 take these same words and demonstrate their use in connected speech. The points to be noted are:

1 not more than one of the syllables that had prominence in the citation form has prominence when the word is used as part of a message
2 which syllable is chosen to be prominent depends upon whether the word is near the beginning or the end of the tone unit
3 if the word is not in a selection slot, neither syllable has prominence.

The possible ways of treating two-prominence words in accordance with these three principles are illustrated in the pyramid diagram that follows Task 9.13.

9.10 ANSWERS

// BARce<u>LO</u>na//   // REfe<u>REE</u> //

9.11 ANSWERS

2 // was MANu<u>FAC</u>ture //   5 // was INter<u>NA</u>tional //
3 // was enVIron<u>MEN</u>tal //   6 // was ARchi<u>TEC</u>turally //
4 // was DEvas<u>TA</u>tion //

➤➤

9.12 ANSWERS

1 // the PROBlem's an environMENtal one //
2 // comPLETE devasTAtion //
3 // sucCESSful archiTECturally //
4 // we must reSTRICT their manuFACture //
5 // TOtally irresPONsible //

9.13 ANSWERS

2 It brings devastation and destruction of our city centres.

3 An architecturally pleasing car park just defies imagination.

4 We need to impose restrictions on their manufacture and use.

5 We simply can't tolerate such irresponsible behaviour.

9.14 and 9.15

These two tasks focus attention upon two separate implications of the 'pyramid' diagram. Firstly, they provide examples of how words which have two prominent syllables in citation forms are treated when they are used – with or without prominence – in connected speech. Secondly, they show how all such syllables retain their full vowel sounds when they are not prominent.

9.14 ANSWERS

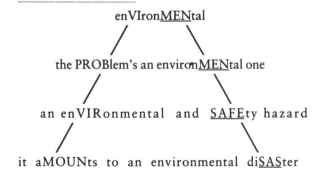

enVIronMENtal

the PROBlem's an environMENtal one

an enVIRonmental and SAFEty hazard

it aMOUNts to an environmental diSASter

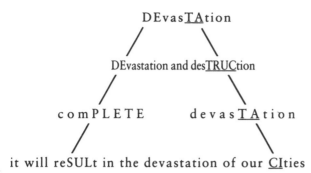

DEvas<u>TA</u>tion

DEvastation and des<u>TRUC</u>tion

comPLETE   devas<u>TA</u>tion

it will reSULt in the devastation of our <u>CI</u>ties

9.15 ANSWERS

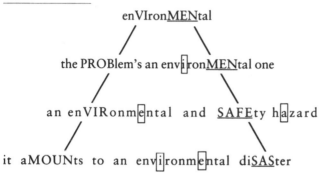

enVIron<u>MEN</u>tal

the PROBlem's an envi ron<u>MEN</u>tal one

an enVIRonm e ntal and <u>SAFE</u>ty h a zard

it aMOUNts to an env i ronm e ntal di<u>SAS</u>ter

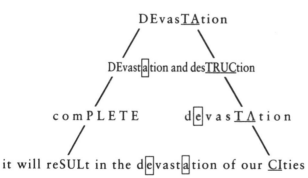

DEvas<u>TA</u>tion

DEvast a tion and des<u>TRUC</u>tion

comPLETE   d e vas<u>TA</u>tion

it will reSULt in the d e vast a tion of our <u>CI</u>ties

9.16

Three of the examples include citation forms.

1 enVIronMENtal
3 IrrePLAce**a**ble
4 ARchiTECturally

In (2) 'environmental' has only one prominence: environMENtal.

Unit 10 Revision: The story so far

Nothing new is introduced in this unit. Each task is intended to provide revision of work covered in one of the earlier units.

Listening for meaning

The preliminary task is intended to ensure that students are thoroughly aware of the participants in the serial and their relationships.

ANSWERS

Morgan was once engaged to Penelope, but when they broke up he went to live in Australia.

Penelope has retired to a cottage on the Suffolk coast after managing a fashion shop near London.

Helen, her daughter, is now the manager of the shop.

Derek, Helen's husband, is a songwriter, who has reasons for wanting to live in London.

Listening to intonation and sounds

10.1–10.5

These tasks provide further experience in using referring and proclaiming tones.

10.1 ANSWERS

1 // ↗ peNElope <u>WAIN</u>wright // ↘ retired to a SEAside <u>CO</u>ttage //
   ↘ on the SUffolk <u>COAST</u> //

2 // ↗ <u>HEL</u>en // ↘ TOOk over the <u>RU</u>nning // ↘ of the <u>SHOP</u> //

3 // ↘ DErek // → aGREED // ↘ ONly // ↗ ON the conDItion //
↘ that they KEEP their FLAt on // ↘ in TOWN //

4 // ↘ an Uninvited GUEST // ↘ at the PARty she had given // ↘ was
MORgan //

10.2 ANSWERS

2 // ↘ MANdy // ↘ was the PERson who rang DAvid // ↘ to ASK
the way to his HOUSE //

3 // ↘ TOM WIlliams // ↘ addressed the NAtional TRANsport
conference // (about, etc.)

4 // ↘ TOny // ↘ was a FORmer COlleague // ↘ of SUE'S // (who,
etc.)

5 // ↘ it was eLIzabeth // (who, etc.)

10.4 ANSWERS

2 // ↘ a LIFE of ARnold // ↘ was the book he WANted //

3 // ↘ the PERson they moved downSTAIRS // ↘ was ARthur //

4 // ↘ it was TOny // ↘ she wanted to SPEAK to //

Proclaiming tones are used with // a LIFE of ARnold //, // was
ARthur // and // it was TOny // as these tone units give the information
asked for in preceding questions.

10.5

This task revises the case of non-prominent syllables which have
protected vowels.

ANSWERS

d[o]ctor soc[i]ety r[a]ng w[ay] addr[e]ssed c[o]nference ab[ou]t
d[a]vid g[a]ve b[oo]k m[o]ved d[ow]n w[a]nted

10.6 and 10.7

These tasks are concerned with the effect of dividing part of the message into more or fewer tone units.

10.7 ANSWERS

Likely to be divided:

4   she left a long time ago
5   the use and manufacture

10.8

In this task students are asked to alternate the use of a fall-rise tone with a rising tone.

2a // ↘↗ but it was NOT without oppoSItion // ↘ from DErek //

2b // ↗ but it was NOT without oppoSItion // ↘ from DErek //

3a // ↘↗ MEANwhile // ↘↗ GOssip has REACHed her // ↘ about what her SOn in law is doing // ↘ in LONdon //

3b // ↗ MEANwhile // ↗ GOssip has REACHed her // ↘ about what her SOn in law is doing // ↘ in LONdon //

4a // ↘ she is reLUCtant // ↘↗ to tell him OUTright // ↘ that he is NOT WELcome //

4b // ↘ she is reLUCtant // ↗ to tell him OUTright // ↘ that he is NOT WELcome //

5a // ↘↗ he TURNed UP // ↘ at the PARty she had given //

5b // ↗ he TURNed UP // ↘ at the PARty she had given //

10.9–10.11

These tasks recall the circumstances in which high and low key are used.

10.9 ANSWERS

There is a step up to high key at 'STILL', 'HOPE' and 'KEEP'.

10.10 ANSWERS

There is a drop down to low key at:

1 <u>HE</u>len
2 <u>SONG</u>writer; <u>HUS</u>band

10.11 ANSWERS

1 high key	5 low key
2 low key	6 high key
3 high key	7 low key
4 high key	

Transcripts

UNIT 1 LISTENING FOR MEANING

It seemed to take an age to get there, but eventually, the bus stopped. We'd got to the terminus and everyone got out. We were somewhere in the commercial district but I wasn't sure where. I couldn't recognise anything. The others hurried off. I hesitated, wondering which way to start. I ought to have asked someone, but it was too late. They'd gone. The street was empty. Even the bus driver had gone. I hurried across and turned into an alleyway and started to walk. It was dark and drizzling a little. I went through an archway and into another street, where there were street lights. It was one of those pedestrian precincts – no cars admitted – with concrete benches to sit on and concrete tubs for plants. But the benches were wet – it was winter – and there wasn't a plant to be seen.

I passed some shops: bright lights and bargains and fashionable dresses on plastic figures, videos, and fridges, and hundreds of shoes at giveaway prices. Leftover gift wrapping and holly and snowmen.

I walked along, looking in the windows. The last of the shop assistants was just closing the doors. Could she tell me, please, where Market Street was? She'd no idea. She was a student, doing a holiday job, and she didn't know the district yet. She thought there was a pub in the first street on the left. Perhaps they'd know there.

It was all very odd. There was just nobody about. I walked on and took the left turning where she'd said, and found the pub, but of course they didn't open till seven, and it was just half past five. I went round to a side door, and rang a bell . . .

UNIT 2 LISTENING FOR MEANING

Mandy: David?
David: Yes.
Mandy: Phoo . . . it's Mandy here.
David: Oh.
Mandy: Hi . . . listen . . . I'm in the Horse and Groom.
David: Good lord! Are you?

Mandy: Yes.
David: You're miles away!
Mandy: I know I'm miles away!
David: Right. Now, you want to know how to get here, I suppose.
Mandy: Well I do.
David: Um.
Mandy: I've got a map, actually, but I think it's dreadfully out of date.
David: Right. Um, well, actually, you come out of the car park . . .
Mandy: Yeah.
David: . . . and really, you should turn left, but you can't because there's that big dual carriageway in the way, so you've got to turn right . . .
Mandy: Turn right out of the car —
David: Yes, are you going to write this down?
Mandy: OK. Turn right out of the car park.
David: Yeah, turn right.
Mandy: Yes.
David: Erm . . . you're on the A703 then.
Mandy: Yeah, that's right.
David: Yeah, right. There's a – hold on – and on your left there's . . . the first turning is a cul-de-sac, and then you will need the next turning – the second turning on the left . . .
Mandy: OK. Hang on . . . second left. Yeah.
David: . . . and you follow the road around . . .
Mandy: Can you . . . yeah, OK. Go on.
David: . . . and there's an underpass, to take you under the trunk road and you keep going along – it's erm . . . it's Hospital Lane – you'll know it's Hospital Lane because of the hospital.
Mandy: Ah. Hospital Lane. Is it Hospital Lane?
David: Hospital Lane.
Mandy: Ah. Because I've been asking for Hospital Road, and they said there isn't one. Right, Hospital Lane.
David: Ah. Well, there's a hospital actually there. It's a big red and yellow brick building.
Mandy: Good. Good. There is one, yeah, yeah.
David: And you go to the end of there. You come to a junction. There's some traffic lights. I think they're under local control 'cause there's an awful lot of . . . You can't go through the centre of town —
Mandy: It's a one-way, isn't it?
David: Huh?

Mandy: It's a one-way?

David: It's . . . well it's one-way at the moment 'cause they're doing a lot of sewer work or something.

Mandy: Now tell me . . . OK. So I go round the one-way system . . .

David: No, no, no, no. It's a set of traffic lights . . .

Mandy: Yeah.

David: Yes. Then you turn right.

Mandy: Yeah.

David: And I think it's – well, actually, the arrows will tell you where to go 'cause it's a diversion – and you turn about – it's about the second turning on the left, and you go . . . er . . . for about fifty yards . . .

Mandy: Yeah.

David: . . . and you come to a main crossroads. I can't remember what happens there. I think there might be some lights there as well . . . but get in the right-hand lane . . .

Mandy: Right-hand lane . . .

David: OK?

Mandy: Yeah.

David: There – it's – there's a Shell service station on the right . . .

Mandy: Yes.

David: . . . and you'll then be in College Lane.

Mandy: College Lane.

David: It's a long – long straight road.

Mandy: OK. And College Lane . . . I go up College Lane.

David: College Lane. You'll see the technical college on your right, and then the primary school . . .

Mandy: Yes.

David: Er . . . and you'll come to a T-junction.

Mandy: Yep.

David: It's quite a big T-junction . . . there's Park Road. Now all this is new. This is all new development. You won't have seen this before. Erm . . . Park Road . . . More lights . . . you turn right . . .

Mandy: OK.

David: Erm . . . until you come to a mini-roundabout, and you want – on the roundabout – you want the first exit . . .

Mandy: Yep.

David: . . . and that's . . . that's Park Close, erm . . .

Mandy: . . . and then I keep going . . . you're on the left, aren't you?

David: We're on the left. Number 27.

Mandy: On the left, number twen— Can you bear to go through that again, quickly? I'll just put another 10p in. OK. Go on. Just

. . . just go through it again, OK. I know I've got to come
out of the car park, turn right . . .

David: Yes, you come out of the car park and turn right.

Mandy: I know how to get to Hospital Lane. I've done that bit
before.

David: You've done that bit before. You can get to Hospital
Lane.

Mandy: Yes.

David: At the traffic lights you turn right.

Mandy: Yes.

David: Erm . . . Second . . . second turning . . . left.

Mandy: Yes, and then I get – keep on that – and get in the right-hand
lane.

David: Yes. Right-hand lane, by the Shell service station.

Mandy: Yes.

David: College Lane, that is.

Mandy: Yes. Past the technical college.

David: Yes. Past the technical college, past the primary school.
Another junction, another T-junction . . . Park Road . . . turn
right.

Mandy: Yep. Take the first exit.

David: First exit at the mini-roundabout.

Mandy: And that's Park Close.

David: That's it.

Mandy: Phoo. OK. See you. Bye.

David? See you in about . . . two minutes.

Mandy: Phoo. You're joking.

2.9

Well you'll have to go back. Go down College Lane, past the technical
college, back to the crossroads. Go straight over there, over the
crossroads, where you've come from. Then turn left into Willow
Road. That's continuing along the road you were on before, and go on
down there until you come to a big roundabout. Take the second exit
and you'll be in a long straight road. Go right to the end and then turn
left, and that will take you to the mini-roundabout you are looking
for, on Park Road.

UNIT 3 LISTENING FOR MEANING

Sue: Cheers!

Tony: Cheers, Sue! Well, what's the news then? How is everybody? I suppose old Arthur's still there. Still trying to keep everyone in order.

Sue: Oh, yeah. He'll go on for ever. Nothing changes for Arthur. Or if it does, he doesn't notice. You remember that friend of his, though, the guy who came from Liverpool . . . He always came on Fridays, and nobody knew quite why.

Tony: Oh that tall guy, yeah. Had an old Bentley or something, didn't he? We used to say he was—

Sue: Yes. Well, nobody knows what happened, but he had a nasty accident of some sort.

Tony: An accident?

Sue: In his car. But you know Arthur – he never tells you much. So we don't really know what it was.

Tony: Oh dear.

Sue: Anyway, he suddenly stopped coming. Rather sad, really.

Tony: What about Jane and Ted, upstairs?

Sue: Ah, well Ted's still there. He's not very happy about it, though. He'd like a move if he could get one, but he sort of seems to be stuck. And Jane – she went about a couple of years ago.

Tony: Really?

Sue: I haven't seen her for ages, so I don't know what she's doing. Nobody seems to be in touch with her. Had Mary come before you left?

Tony: Mary who?

Sue: Mary in Accounts. She's Irish.

Tony: I don't think so, no. I knew Sarah. I remember she was in Accounts. And then there was that other Jane, Jane Harrison. And then there was Angela, of course, the rather serious one. But I don't recall a Mary.

Sue: Well, she must have been after you left, then.

Tony: Did she replace that man who got moved to Head Office? What was his name, now? He left round about the same time as I did. There was a bit of a fuss about it because a lot of people—

Sue: Oh, you mean John Fellows – oh, they say he's doing very well, incidentally. No, no, no. This was much later. It was some time after John went. No, you wouldn't have known her I expect. Oh well, there's not much point in telling you about her, is there – only there was quite a storm about it at the time . . .

3.2

Sue: You know everything's been changed now, I suppose?
Tony: Has it?
Sue: Mm, the second floor's completely different. It's all open plan now. They've opened it all up completely. Bit more friendly, really. Those three little offices that were there – you know what it used to be like – well, they've gone.
Tony: I can't remember what it was like, really. Erm . . . that's where the coffee room was, wasn't it?
Sue: Yeah.
Tony: Wait a minute . . . there was the post room . . .
Sue: Mm.
Tony: . . . and then there was Arthur's place . . . and there was the photocopying room. So where's Arthur now?
Sue: They've given him a room downstairs. Oh, and you wouldn't recognise the reception area. You know that horrible corridor we had?
Tony: Oh yeah.
Sue: And the little room where the stove was?
Tony: Yeah.
Sue: Well it's all gone. It's all plush carpet and easy chairs down there now.
Tony: No!
Sue: And there's a vending machine there now too. We have to go down there for our coffee!
Tony: Oh, I bet you don't like that.
Sue: Well no, not really. I suppose it's not as friendly as the old coffee room was. But it's not too bad. Seems a long time since those days now.
Tony: Yeah.
Sue: I've nearly forgotten what it was like when you and Jane and everybody were around. Oh, there's a sort of sitting room off to the left, too – we usually manage a chat in there if we're not too busy . . .

UNIT 4 LISTENING FOR MEANING

Conversation 1
Bookseller: Good morning. Can I help you?
Customer: I'm looking for a book by Sutcliffe. It's *A Life of Arnold*.
Bookseller: *A Life of Arnold*. Let me see, now. Is that the title?
Customer: I think so.

Bookseller: It isn't the title of a novel?

Customer: Well, I don't think it is. But the problem is, I'm not quite sure.

Bookseller: I see. You've looked in the biography section?

Customer: Is that near the maps and things? Over there?

Bookseller: That's right.

Customer: Yes, I've looked there. But I can't see it.

Bookseller: You don't know who the publisher is?

Customer: Sorry, no.

Bookseller: Would you mind waiting a moment, while I serve this lady, and then I'll see what I can do for you.

Customer: Thank you.

Conversation 2

Traveller: Can you help me, please? I'm travelling to York, but apparently, the train I was going to catch has been cancelled.

Assistant: The train to York. When were you hoping to travel?

Traveller: On the eleven forty-eight. And on the indicator board it says it's cancelled.

Assistant: Eleven forty-eight to York. That's right. There seems to be some trouble on the line . . . they've had to take it off. The next direct train is at thirteen twenty.

Traveller: Thirteen twenty. And when does it get to York?

Assistant: It gets to York . . . at . . . fifteen ten.

Traveller: Oh, Lord! Perhaps I could go by another route, by an earlier train?

Assistant: Just a moment. How much luggage do you have?

Traveller: Only this bag.

Assistant: Because if you don't mind changing, you could go via Manchester. There's a train due out in – hang on – just five minutes.

Traveller: Which platform will that be?

Assistant: From platform two. But you'll have to change.

Traveller: I don't mind that. But what about my ticket? Can I use the same ticket?

Assistant: Let me look. That's OK, yes. It's just the same fare.

Traveller: And what time will that get me there?

Assistant: At fourteen forty-eight. About twenty minutes before the direct train. But you'll have to hurry. Platform two – change at Manchester.

Traveller: Thanks!

UNIT 5 LISTENING FOR MEANING

Er . . . good evening. Er . . . good evening to one and all. Welcome to our February meeting. Erm . . . and welcome of course to our . . . to our regular members and attenders and several faces er . . . I can see out there not too familiar to me, and if you're new and here for the first time a great welcome, and I hope you may consider joining us on a . . . on a more permanent basis.

Erm . . . before I introduce tonight's speaker there's er . . . one important reminder. Erm . . . next month's meeting at the same time will be our annual general meeting and er . . . on that occasion we're hoping for a good and spirited attendance and there's some urgent pieces of business to attend to on that occasion. Er . . . first and foremost and probably the most important is to elect a new secretary. Er . . . Jane Parks has served us marvellously for – I think it's about three years now – er . . . our present secretary – she's leaving to take up a post in Glasgow. We wish her well, erm . . . and any suggestions for replacing Jane before that meeting would be most welcome.

Erm . . . several committee members have also expressed a wish to stand down, for one reason or another, pressure of business and so on, and will need to be replaced so there'll be elections for them. Erm . . . also, and this is rather a sad note, the treasurer tells me that we must seriously consider increasing subscriptions – not a . . . not a happy thing to suggest at this time of the year – but we erm . . . we are, in fact, er . . . going into the red in a rather serious way. So erm . . . that's something to bear in mind for next month's meeting.

Erm . . . as these things are very important, we need as many of you here as possible to make the decisions about these matters. Unfortunately today, our attendance, I can see, is not as good as usual, erm . . . possibly due to the flu epidemic and erm . . . and . . . and the storms and unseasonal weather outside. A number of people rang to say they didn't think they'd be able to make it and er . . . I won't read out apologies for absence, we'll just take their word for it.

And now, erm . . . the most important business of this evening is for me to introduce today's speaker, er . . . Doctor Agnes Thomson, no stranger to us as you will remember her stimulating paper on the Tractatus. I think it was about three years ago, if I'm not much mistaken.

Erm . . . for the benefit of the others, erm . . . who didn't hear her on that occasion, erm . . . just a few words about her background. She graduated from this university before getting her master's degree and subsequently her doctorate at Harvard in the United States and erm . . . has since acquired a distinguished reputation on both sides of the Atlantic. Everyone er . . . familiar with our discipline will know of her many contributions er . . . to the literature. We look forward to her book. She says it should hopefully be out in the autumn, and er . . . she's recently returned to us from a year in India. She taught philosophy at the University of Hyderabad. Anyway, on to her topic for tonight. It's called 'Language Games or Power Games: Wittgenstein and the Feminist Perspective'.

Ladies and gentlemen, Dr Agnes Thomson.

UNIT 6 LISTENING FOR MEANING

Jane: Norton five nine seven.

Susan: Jane. Susan here.

Jane: Hi, Susan. How are things?

Susan: Fine. Pretty busy, as usual. How about you?

Jane: OK. Pretty good, really. Did you want to talk to Tony?

Susan: Is he there?

Jane: Well, no. Actually, it's his day in London, today. It's nearly always on Tuesdays, these days. He'll be back this evening, though.

Susan: You don't know what time this evening?

Jane: Well, he's usually in about six.

Susan: OK.

Jane: Is there anything I can do? Get him to ring back or anything?

Susan: Would you mind? Only there's something I've got to sort out with him. I suppose I could leave it till I see him on Thursday at the meeting. Tonight would be better, though.

Jane: Will you be at home or at the office?

Susan: Erm . . . hang on a minute. I shall have to think about that. If he could possibly make it about seven . . . I'll certainly be home by then. Or perhaps it would be better if I called him?

Jane: No, don't worry. He's sure to be here at seven. I'll tell him. Don't worry.

Susan: Thanks, Jane. Are you going to be there on Friday?

Jane: Ooh, hope so, if the babysitter doesn't let us down.

Susan: See you then.

Jane: Sure.

Susan: Bye now.

Jane: Bye.

UNIT 7 LISTENING FOR MEANING

I'd been shopping, you know, and it was getting late. And I'd left the car in that erm . . . that multi-storey car park just off Hurst Street. And when I got out of the lift, I looked across, and I thought there was someone sitting in the passenger seat, you know. So I thought, 'Well, that's odd. I couldn't have locked it properly.' And then I wondered, 'Well, what am I going to do now?' I mean, you know. (*bleep*)

Well anyway, they saw me coming because the door opened and this person got out, and it was a little old lady with a shopping bag. And er . . . and she said, 'I hope you don't mind, but I've arranged to meet my daughter here, and I started to feel ever so giddy.' So then she said she just had to sit in my car. 'Well,' I said, 'when was your daughter supposed to be coming?' and she said 'Half an hour ago. Er . . . I can't think what's happened to her. She's never been late like this before.' So I said, 'Where do you live?' And she said she was going back to her daughter's and er . . . then she said, 'Would it be going out of your way to drop me near there?' (*bleep*)

Well, there was nothing I could do. I thought, 'I can't leave her standing here.' Apart from anything else, it was very cold outside – it was that . . . that very cold time we had in February – you know, and she looked perfectly awful. So, well I had no choice. I told her to get in the car and I decided to drive her to her daughter's. Anyway, as we were driving along, she was very, very still and quiet and it sort of worried me a bit. And I kept saying, 'Are you OK?' and er . . . she'd mutter something, you know. And as the traffic got a bit easier, I managed to look across at her, and she was shuffling about a bit, and then she took out one of her hands, out from underneath her coat. And as soon as I saw it, I thought, 'That's not a woman's hand.' She covered it up straight away, but I could see that it was big and it was hairy. Then I looked down at her shoes, and at the side of her face, and I could see that I was truly in a situation. So I thought, 'What am I going to do now?' (*bleep*)

As it happened, we were just coming up to a big roundabout, and I deliberately went past the exit we needed and took the next one. And she said, 'Sorry, dear, but wasn't that the road?'

'Oh yes,' I said, 'Yeah. It was. How stupid of me! It's a long time since I came this way,' and I said, 'I have to turn around,' to her.

And a bit further along the road, there was this narrow drive on the left. So I stopped, and I said, 'Er . . . look, I'm not very good at this sort of thing. Erm . . . would you mind just getting out and seeing me back into that drive?' So anyway, he got out with his bag and everything, and went round to the back of the car, and as soon as the door was closed, I swung smartly round, and accelerated off just as fast as I could to the police station!

Well, I told them what had happened, and they said erm . . . , 'Can we borrow your keys, because we'd like to go out and search your car.'

And when they came back, they asked me if I could tell them what was in the car, and I thought, and I thought there was my shopping but I didn't think that there was anything else. And then they said, 'Well, are you sure that's all?' And they kept saying, 'Think hard.' And I said, 'No, I'm sure that's all.' Anyway in the end they just told me: 'We found an axe down beside the rear seat.'

UNIT 8 LISTENING FOR MEANING

Interviewer: Among the speakers at today's National Transport Conference will be Mr Tom Williams. Mr Williams, I understand that, having been a keen, not to say fanatical, motorist for most of your life, you're now having second thoughts?

Mr Williams: That's quite correct, yes.

Interviewer: And what exactly is it that you'll be saying to the conference?

Mr Williams: It's a very simple message, really. I'm saying we should restrict the manufacture and use of private motor cars and er . . . concentrate instead on developing efficient and cheap public transport.

Interviewer: Can you explain to us why you feel so strongly about this? (*bleep*)

Mr Williams: Well, I think first and foremost there's . . . there's what I call the environmental case. Er . . . we all know that cars consume valuable energy sources . . . resources. They produce carbon dioxide in great quantities and they're major contributors to environmental problems. Er . . . for instance, their manufacture uses up other scarce, often irreplaceable, natural resources, and erm . . . they're essentially . . . they're essentially short-lived articles. They create continuing and ever-increasing problems of disposal when they're no longer wanted.

Interviewer: But if we had to rely on public transport as you're suggesting, well shouldn't we lose a great deal in the way of mobility and freedom to go where we please?

Mr Williams: Well, er . . . I mean it must be obvious to everybody that traffic congestion has already reached crisis proportions in many places. Now this, in itself, effectively reduces the very mobility that cars are supposed to promote. And there's the need to accommodate them in towns and er . . . to provide for parking for them, now overriding all other considerations in town planning. I mean can you, can you show me a multi-storey car park that is architecturally beautiful? I'm sure you can't. Now the result is erm . . . there's devastation and dehumanisation of many of our urban centres. Erm . . . and even if you stray away from the towns – out of town for instance . . . the trunk roads and motorways, we hear complaints about this every day, rapidly eating into the rural landscape, affecting the quality of life, people who live in the country, and of course threatening wildlife itself.

Interviewer: And presumably you have in mind also the risk to life and limb that the motor car represents?

Mr Williams: Indeed I do. Er . . . you see advertising pressures in the motor industry . . . they emphasise . . . they emphasise speed, they emphasise performance, and worst of all they emphasise these qualities under a banner of being able to do it safely. Do you see what I mean? Erm . . . you can be heroically dangerous and do it safely if you've got good tyres or good brakes, and this in itself incites all kinds of showing off, all encourage irresponsible and aggressive behaviour, especially in the young. And apart from the resulting tragic injury and loss of life, the resulting accidents make enormous demands on medical services, which could be better employed in other ways.

Interviewer: But Mr Williams, aren't you overlooking the economic aspect of the thing? I mean our prosperity as a nation like that of Japan, for instance, seems to be so tightly bound up with our ability to make and sell cars. Can we really hope to reverse all this?

Mr Williams: Well, quite frankly, I regard this as the most serious aspect of all. It . . . it's all an illusion. The seemingly limitless mass market for motor cars has distorted the economies of advanced countries in particular. It's come to be seen as . . . as essential for maintaining an acceptable level of employment. Now I have to agree that disengaging ourselves from . . . from . . . from . . . this is never going to be easy. The longer this goes on the greater will be the problem of trying to change it without creating economic and social chaos. And it doesn't only concern us. There's an international dimension to all of this. You see there's an understandable desire on the part of the still-developing countries to get in on the act and follow us in putting what is our dream of the universal motor car ownership before other economic objectives, which in their case should be given higher priority.

Interviewer: So what you're saying, Mr Williams, is that they would do better to learn from our mistakes than follow our examples?

Mr Williams: That's precisely what I'm saying.

Interviewer: Mr Williams, thank you very much. That was Mr Tom Williams, who will be addressing the National Transport Conference in London this afternoon.

UNIT 9 LISTENING FOR MEANING

In Barcelona today, supporters clashed, when England played their World Cup match against Spain, the present cup holders. England had held the champions to one-one until half time, but soon after play was resumed a penalty was awarded against them. According to our reporter, Jim Bullock, the decision caused uproar among a group of England fans, and this in turn triggered an angry response from some opposing supporters in an adjoining section of the stand.

The referee stopped the game when violence spilled over onto the pitch, and there were several minutes of noisy confusion until local police restored order and escorted alleged ringleaders out of the stadium. Apparently, there were further disturbances in pavement cafés and bars in town after the match. No one seems to have been injured seriously, either inside or outside the stadium. It is not known whether the police made any arrests. After order had been restored on the pitch, England attacked vigorously, but the Spanish defence was too well disciplined for them, and their hopes of appearing in the final were dashed when the opposition captain, Marcos, scored the winning goal, just thirty seconds before time.

UNIT 10 LISTENING FOR MEANING

After giving up the management of her successful fashion store in the Home Counties, Penelope Wainwright retired to a seaside cottage on the Suffolk coast. Her daughter, Helen, took over the running of the shop; but it was not without a certain amount of opposition from Derek, her songwriter husband. Derek, who, at thirty-two, has still not lost hope of making the big time in the entertainment world, agreed only on the condition that they keep their flat on in town as a base for his professional activities.

For Penelope, retirement promises to be more eventful than she'd bargained for. An uninvited guest at the party she had given, just before she left for the cottage, was Morgan, a one-time commercial traveller, to whom she had been engaged in the days when she was still a sales assistant. Embittered and disillusioned by his experiences in Australia, where he went after he and Penelope had decided to go their separate ways, he has since turned up a number of times in Suffolk. These visits have excited the interest of her neighbours, and although Penelope is reluctant to tell him outright that he is not welcome, she is finding his attentions embarrassing, and an obstacle to her settling down in her new life.

Meanwhile, gossip has reached her, via a former business associate, that her son-in-law is using the London base for other activities than strictly professional ones.